Preparing Teens for the Contemporary Workforce

Reproducible Masters For Teaching Life Skills and Career Development

Dianne Schilling

Pat Schwallie-Giddis

W. James Giddis

Many thanks to Emily Reisch for her contributions to the introduction of this book.

Illustrations: Dianne Schilling

Copyright © 2011, Innerchoice Publishing • All rights reserved

Portions of this book were previously published in *Preparing Teens for the World of Work*, Copyright, 1995, Innerchoice Publishing

ISBN – 10: 1-56499-071-6

ISBN – 13: 978-1-56499-071-6

INNERCHOICE Publishing
15079 Oak Chase Court
Wellington, FL 33414

www.InnerchoicePublishing.com

Before everything else,
getting ready is the secret to success.

Henry Ford

Table of Contents

Introduction

The world today is complex and rapidly changing. With significant changes in social, political, economic, and technological aspects of society, the vast majority of young people are ill prepared for the real world, particularly the world of work. They will experience difficulty in making the transition from school to work and then will continue experiencing challenges transitioning from one job to another throughout life. These students, fresh from sequestered rows of desks with passing "basic skills" aren't prepared for the rapidly changing workplace. With little guidance, direction, or support, they move from job to job. A fortunate few eventually stumble upon a career path, find a direction, and are able to achieve success. The rest are still struggling to navigate and survive in the real world.

Our young people need to be taught to be adaptable, flexible, and resourceful in the face of changing trends, which include:
- The increase in computer technology
- The increase in part time, temporary, and seasonal positions
- The increase in the number of women and minorities in the work force
- The increase in low-paying positions, unemployment and under-employment
- The increase in the number of job changes expected during a lifetime
- The shift from the production/ manufacturing sector, to the service sector, and now into the information and technology age

Career development should be viewed as a life-long process of acquiring the knowledge, skills, and attitudes that encourage success in life as well as the ability to transition from school to the world of work. Young people need to be directly and purposefully taught the skills and knowledge necessary for life success. Its acquisition is not an instinctive process but rather one of repeated exposure and practice.

Career development in the form of career education and career guidance, has been in existence for some time, but it is typically not a part of the core curriculum in schools today. Critical job-finding and job-keeping skills should be integral to educational curriculum and taught in a deliberate fashion. Today's career development programs should aim to provide skills, attitudes and knowledge students need in order to succeed in the world of the 21st century.

Let's Clarify Terms

The word career refers to more than a person's current job or occupation. A career is a sequence of occupations and other life roles that combine to express one's commitment to work within the total pattern of self-development. The terms career development, career guidance and career counseling are often used interchangeably. While they are closely related, there are critical differences among them.

• **Career development** is an evolutionary process that begins in childhood and extends through adulthood. It is the process by which one develops and refines self- and career-identity, work maturity and the ability to plan. It represents all the career-related choices and outcomes through which every person must pass. Indeed career development is generally conceived as a lifelong process through which individuals come to understand themselves as they relate to the world of work and their role in it.

• **Career guidance** is an intervention. Intended to assist individuals to manage their career development, career guidance is a program of counselor-coordinated information, experiences, and support services to help students gain understanding of their social, intellectual, and emotional development; become knowledgeable about educational, occupational, and social opportunities; learn decision-making and planning skills; and combine these insights into personal plans of action.

• **Career counseling** in schools is based on the continuous development of theories, processes, and practice in career development. It involves communication that takes place between counseling professionals and students concerning issues of preferences, competency, achievement, self-esteem and the array of factors that facilitate personal career planning.

• **Career education** (a term used more in the 1970s than it is today) is conceptually very much like comprehensive career guidance, although career education programs tend to place greater emphasis on the teaching/learning process as presented by classroom teachers whereas, in career guidance, the school counselor is the key delivery person.

Counselor Driven

Career development, in its most inclusive sense, involves everyone, and successfully preparing young people for work is an attitude that pervades the home, school, business and social community. Teachers, students, parents, employers, career specialists, school administrators, and community leaders all have important roles to play. However, in this book we view the monumental task of initiating and sustaining a school-to-work concept through the uniquely calibrated lens of the school counselor.

The Design of This Book

Preparing Teens for the Contemporary Workforce has been designed to assist counselors and career specialist in their efforts to prepare today's students for success in a dynamic workplace that demands ever increasing and changing skills. These skills are divided into two primary areas.

Job Finding Skills

The student worksheets in this section are designed to help students acquire three of the most obvious yet frequently neglected sets of job-finding skills. They prepare students to:
- Conduct focused, thorough, creative job searches
- Write and maintain effective resumes
- Prepare for and successfully manage job interviews.

Job search skills, resume writing, and interviewing are three skills that need to be addressed as a component of a comprehensive career development program. All high-school students, regardless of their individual career goals, will benefit from developing a beginning resume and becoming accustomed to the practice of maintaining this printed reflection of their accomplishments , experiences, and occupational objectives. All students need to know that a successful job search involves much more than simply scanning the classified ads or doing an online job search. Students will be facing a future with multiple career-related interviews and this book will assist them in this process.

Job Keeping Skills

The student worksheets in this section address some of the skills and attributes desired most by employers:
- Attitude
- Appearance
- Attendance
- Communication
- Following directions
- Productivity and time management
- Respecting authority
- Teamwork and cooperation
- Appreciation for coworkers
- Customer service
- Decision- making
- Completing assignments
- Initiative
- Problem solving
- Handling criticism
- Assertiveness
- Conflict-Resolution
- Trustworthiness
- Independence

The knowledge and skills learned through these worksheets and your instruction will benefit students in their school life and will literally be carried later to their work place where the learnings will be applied. Students will be acquiring highly desirable workplace competencies, which are proven strategies for job and life success.

How to Use This Book

The activity sheets in Preparing Teens for the Contemporary Workforce are written in a conversational style, and speak directly to the individual student. Since many of you are counselors and career specialists working with individual students, we wanted you to be able to hand the sheets out on an individual basis. For the most part, they require little or no advance explanation from you; however, you are strongly encouraged to spend some time going over them with the student after they have been completed. Although the activity sheets are written for the individual, using them with groups can be equally effective. Many of the activity sheets lend themselves to further discussion, exploration, and role-playing. Have the students get together in dyads, triads and/or small groups to discuss their completed worksheets. Use the activities to generate discussion. Select specific activities and have the students collaborate in following the instructions and answering questions.

We hope that you will enjoy working with these materials and find them useful. The reactions of the students to the various topic areas will undoubtedly spark many ideas for additional activities and areas of inquiry.

Job Finding Skills

Finding a Job That's Just Right for You

Target:

The activities in this section will help you:

⇨ explore the most effective job search methods.

⇨ specify your skills and career goals.

⇨ identify preferred industries and companies

⇨ devote time to informational interviewing

⇨ answer ads and fill out applications

⇨ use tips for a successful career search.

Favorite Job-search Methods

As a job seeker, you can choose from a variety of methods while conducting your search. Below is a list of the approaches that people have used to find jobs. The list is ranked in order of the *success* of the methods, not popularity. In fact, the most popular method — using the want ads — is actually one of the less effective methods.

• Research and networking/referral
• Applying *in person* directly to the employer
• Asking friends and relatives about job openings
• Responding to want ads
• Using school or placement services
• Professional and trade organizations
• Using state Bureau of Employment Services

You can also find out about job openings by checking with:

—state public employment service offices
—civil service announcements
—local and out-of-town newspapers
—professional journals
—trade magazines
—armed forces recruiting agencies

—labor unions
—professional associations
—libraries and community centers
—women's counseling and employment programs
—youth programs
—school placement services
—employment agencies and career consultants

Commit to Using the Most Effective Method

The method with the highest rate of success is the creative combination of research/contact and networking/referral. Research/contact involves the following:

1. Doing *self-research* to discover everything you can about *you* — your skills, likes, dislikes, values, attributes, preferences, talents, etc.
2. Doing *job/career* research to learn about many different industries, occupations, and careers.
3. Matching yourself to two or three specific jobs/careers.
4. Identifying companies that offer these jobs/careers.
5. Contacting key people in those companies to get more information about the identified jobs/careers.
6. Asking those people for referrals to other companies and their key people.
7. As a result of these "informational interviews," zeroing in on two or three companies where you would like to work.
8. Applying directly to those companies.

The second element is word-of-mouth networking/referral. This means developing a list of contacts and then letting them know that you are looking for a job and just what kind of job you want. Most people like helping others. With a large group of people thinking of you and the type of job you want, when a job opening comes up, they will very likely let you know and will often be willing to provide you with a referral. This gives you a very good chance of getting the job you want. It's really important to keep in touch with your contacts by phone, email, or in person, and to keep them informed of the progress of your job search.

Anyone you know, or anyone who knows someone you know, can be a potential contact in your network. Think big. Consider your family, friends, your extended family and even the families of your friends—teachers, coaches, counselors, administrators and anyone in any organization to which you belong. Get the picture? *They all belong in your network.*

(On a separate sheet start making a list of all these people.)

What Are Your Favorite Skills?

Skills are the building blocks of any career. They are what all jobs and all careers have in common. You have learned many skills in school, and you can transfer those from the classroom to a job, and from one job to another.

Skills are best described using *action* words. Here are some examples:

keeping records	writing	repairing
gathering information	tutoring	constructing
problem solving	entertaining	cooking
planning	playing an instrument	tending
computing	leading	assembling/setting up
drawing	communicating effectively	driving

Skills break down into three families, those that you use in working with **People**, those that you use in working with **Data and Information**, and those that you use in working with **Things**.

Think back over the things you have accomplished during your lifetime — particularly in school and any jobs you've held. Try to identify the skills you've learned. (If you're still not sure what a skill is, ask your counselor or teacher for assistance.)

Skills with People	Skills with Data/Information	Skills with Things

Go back and choose your five favorite skills. Number them **1** through **5**.

What Are Your Career Goals?

Understanding yourself is an important part of knowing what jobs you will find satisfying and what career goals you should pursue. Job satisfaction and general happiness depend a great deal on your job aligning with your interests.

In working with your counselor, you've most likely taken various tests and assessments to help identify your skills, aptitudes, likes and dislikes. Based on all of this research, what jobs/careers would you like to explore?

Job/Career Options

Job Title 1: _____

Description: _____

_____

Job Title 2: _____

Description: _____

_____

Job Title 3: _____

Description: _____

_____

Identifying Industries and Companies

There are many different types of jobs and careers in practically every area of business and industry. The following is a list of major industries within which there are hundreds of different categories of jobs.

Industries:

_____ Advertising and Public Relations

_____ Aerospace

_____ Agriculture

_____ Automotive

_____ Aviation

_____ Banking

_____ Broadcasting

_____ Chemicals

_____ Computers and Electronics

_____ Education

_____ Energy

_____ Fashion

_____ Film and Entertainment

_____ Financial Services

_____ Food/Beverage Services

_____ Health Services and Pharmaceuticals

_____ Hospitality

_____ Insurance

_____ IT (Information Technology)

_____ Manufacturing

_____ Metals and Mining

_____ Paper and Forest Products

_____ Publishing

_____ Real Estate and Construction

_____ Retailing

_____ Telecommunications

_____ Transportation

_____ Travel

_____ Utilities

Within each industry or career field, you can find jobs that deal primarily with people, primarily with information/data, or primarily with things. Within the broad category of Banking, for example, you could work as a teller or investment counselor (with people), as a financial analyst (with information/data), or as an ATM installer/technician (with things). Many jobs involve working with a combination of the three areas, but most jobs emphasize one. Put a check (✔) in front of the industries that you would like to learn more about.

Use the lines below to list three industries you have decided to explore and some companies that you will contact in those industries. To find companies that employ people in the occupation you have chosen, check these resources:

- ✔ your school's career center
- ✔ yellow pages
- ✔ newspaper want ads
- ✔ chamber of commerce
- ✔ friends and relatives
- ✔ libraries
- ✔ employment agencies
- ✔ internet

Industry:_____

Companies in this industry:

_____

_____

_____

Industry:_____

Companies in this industry:

_____

_____

_____

Industry:_____

Companies in this industry:

_____

_____

_____

Informational Interviewing

You should schedule plenty of Informational interviews before you actually start applying for jobs. Remember, this type of interview is an important part of your research. Its purpose is *not* to ask for a job. You are there to gather information, bring your target into sharper focus, and increase your alternatives. Each informational interview gives you:

1. a new contact for your network
2. first-hand information about the company
3. a clear idea of how your job goal fits within that company
4. additional choices/alternatives
5. practice interviewing
6. referrals to other companies and individuals

When you request an interview, ask for 20 minutes of the person's time and stick to it. Begin the interview by talking briefly about your skills and the sort of career you are preparing for. Then ask the person to tell you about the company and about jobs within the company that someone like you might fit. Ask questions, answer questions, and take notes.

Before you leave, request at least one referral — an individual in another organization whom you can contact, using this person's name. Always follow up within 24 hours with a thank-you note, just as you do after a job interview. For your own use complete a **Company Information Sheet** on every company you visit.

Company Information Sheet

Duplicate this form and complete one sheet on every company you research and/or visit.

Name of Company: _____

Address: _____

Website: _____

Contact(s): _____ Phone # _____

Email: _____

Key information (products, customers, size, history, number of employees, problems, growth, etc.):

_____

_____

_____

_____

Questions to ask in an informational interview:

1. _____

2. _____

3. _____

4. _____

Possible jobs to apply for:

_____

_____

_____

How/to whom to apply: _____

_____

_____

Answering the Ads

Study the job advertisements in newspapers and on the internet thoroughly and on a regular basis. This may not be the best way to find a job, but you need to use *all* the methods you can. Besides, you can learn other things by reading want ads. You can identify companies that you didn't know about, and you can begin to see which companies are doing a lot of hiring.

Want ads are alphabetized by job title and often contain abbreviations and unfamiliar language. (Another thing you can learn by reading want ads is useful job-hunting vocabulary.)

The best ads to answer are the ones that give the most information: company name and address, job title, exact qualifications, information about the company's products and services, etc. If you see a job for which you might qualify, even a little, send your resume, or resume and cover letter, or just a cover letter.

Employers receive from 20 to 1000 resumes and/or letters for each job opening they announce. It takes 48 to 96 hours for the resumes, letters, and emails to reach the employer. The third day after the opening is announced is usually the peak day. Sending your response on the fourth day or later may put you at a slight advantage, because your response will end up near the top of the stack.

Quote the announcement's specifications, and tailor your resume and/or cover letter so that you fit the specifications as closely as possible. Omit all clsc from your response, so there will be little excuse for screening you out.

Don't mention salary. (Asking for too much or too little may cause you to be screened out.) If the ad requests salary requirements, either ignore it, or write something like, "depending on the nature and scope of duties and responsibilities."

Applying Yourself

In addition to accepting your resume and cover letter, many companies require that you fill out a standard application form. Take the time to complete the form accurately and clearly. This will help you make a good impression. Your prospective employer may have many applications, so yours must *stand out*.

An application that is not neat and legible reflects a very poor image of the writer. Take the extra time to be neat and careful. Here are some tips:

Read the directions. Failure to follow the directions on the application may give a prospective employer the impression that you are careless about directions in general.

Get organized. Be sure you have all the necessary and correct information, including exact names and addresses of companies you have worked for, correct employment dates, and the names, titles, addresses and phone numbers of your references.

Print, do not write. If the application is a hard copy and not online, use a black or blue ball point pen rather than a pencil.

Answer every question. If a question does not apply to you, write N.A. (not applicable).

Be honest. Many companies will fire you if they find out that you have been dishonest on a job application.

Be neat. Allow yourself plenty of time. Avoid smudges, smears, and scratch outs.

Spell correctly. If you have any doubts about your spelling ability, use a dictionary or spell checker.

Be specific about the job you want. Use the correct job title. If you are interested in more than one position, separate applications may be required.

Don't specify salary. There is only one answer to the salary question: OPEN

Developing Alternatives

• Learn to describe what you do (or want to do) in different words. Companies tend to develop unique vocabularies. The more ways you can describe your skills, the greater your chances of sounding like a good fit.

• Learn to describe yourself in terms of your skills, rather than your target job title. Remember, skills are *transferable* from one job to another.

• Make a long list of alternative employers. Don't fall in love with an "ideal" company and pin all your hopes on finding employment there.

• Identify different fields and companies that might utilize a person with your interests and aptitudes.

• Consider alternative forms of employment, such as part-time jobs, flexible shifts and hours, and employment through a temporary agency (an agency that services a variety of companies, placing workers in short-term, temporary jobs).

Guaranteeing Your Success

Here are some additional tips that can give you the edge in finding exactly the right job.

- **Use as many job-hunting methods as possible.**
While you're conducting your research and referral search, continue to check newspaper and trade journal want ads and internet job sites daily, and visit employment offices and placement services on a regular basis. Remind friends and relatives to keep their eyes and ears open.

- **Spend more hours a week on your job search.**
Treat your job search like a regular job. If you are in school, consider it an after-school job.

- **Visit more employers each week.**
If you are not in school, visit at least two potential employers a day. This is true for informational interviews as well as job interviews. If you have classes and homework, try to fit in two interviews a week.

- **Apply at small companies.**
Small businesses account for the great majority of new jobs created each year. Search out companies with 25 or fewer employees. Companies of 200 or less are considered small.

- **Find or create a support group.**
Stay in close touch with your counselor. If possible, join a career-counseling group at your school and attend sessions regularly. Your peers will give you lots of support and encouragement and you can do the same for them.

Writing a Winning Resume

You on the Printed Page

A resume is a snapshot of you. It lets employers know what you have to offer and provides them with a clear picture of your experience and qualifications. Resumes work best when used as "calling cards." At the conclusion of an in-person contact with a prospective employer, leave a resume as a summary of you and a reminder of your visit. Other ways to use your resume include:

• Send a resume in response to a want ad.
• Send a resume as a way of introducing yourself to any company that interests you.

When mailed, a resume should be accompanied by a cover letter. The cover letter allows you to strike up a dialog with the prospective employer, which you cannot do with a resume alone. Sample cover letters are included later in this section.

Try to limit your resume to one page. When responding to want ads, take time to tailor your resume to the specific requirements of the advertised job. This is a fairly easy task if you save all versions of your resume on a computer.

Target:

The activities in this section will help you:

⇨ understand the purposes and uses of a resume.

⇨ use action words to capture the vitality of your experiences.

⇨ identify and describe your accomplishments.

⇨ use samples and worksheets to write a draft of your resume.

⇨ write introductory and want-ad response letters.

Make Your Resume Action Packed

Use *action words* in your resume to describe your skills, accomplishments, and the duties and responsibilities you have fulfilled in school and employment. For example:

As assistant manager, I supervised 6 sales people.

Received and directed patients, scheduled appointments, answered telephone, processed payments, and maintained physician calendars.

In the previous section, "Finding the Job That's Just Right for You," you used action words ending in "ing" to describe your skills (*problem solving, planning, computing, drawing, writing*). On your resume, most of the action words will end in "ed" because they refer to *past* accomplishments and activities. Here are some examples:

adapted	established	participated	researched
administered	expanded	performed	revamped
analyzed	evaluated	pinpointed	scheduled
approved	expedited	presented	set up
completed	founded	programmed	simplified
conceived	generated	proposed	solved
conducted	implemented	proved	streamlined
controlled	improved	reduced	structured
coordinated	interpreted	recommended	supervised
created	invented	reinforced	supported
delegated	launched	reorganized	sold
developed	led	repaired	taught
directed	originated	requested	trained

The Parts of a Resume

In the course of a year, an employer may receive hundreds, even thousands of resumes. Every single one is different, yet all are similar. There is no "magic" formula for a resume, because you never know what is going to impress (or turn off) an individual employer. Concentrate on making your resume concise, accurate, attractive, and easy to read. Here are some general guidelines of the things to include in your resume:

Objective statement: An objective statement describes the type of position you are seeking. If you know exactly what you want to do, include an objective statement. If you are hoping that employers will consider you for more than one type of position, omit the objective statement. Notice how short and specific these sample objective statements are:

Sales representative in cosmetics at a major department store.

Medical records clerk in a physician office, clinic, or hospital.

Entry-level position in computer-graphics design for advertising/marketing firm.

Summary statement: A summary statement is two to four sentences long and briefly summarizes your qualifications. Mention work experience, skills, special abilities, talents, and personal traits. Depending on the job you are seeking, you might also want to list equipment and computer hardware and software with which you are proficient.

Accomplishment statements: An accomplishment is anything that you have done that has made a *positive difference* for you or others, and especially for an employer or organization, like your school. An accomplishment might be a problem you solved, an improvement you made, a goal you accomplished, a procedure you developed, or a product you created. Employers are particularly impressed by accomplishments that save money, time, or resources, or boost earnings.

Accomplishment statements are one sentence in length and usually start with an *action* word, like those on the previous list. They briefly describe what you did and the benefits of your action. Here are some samples:

Maintained a 3.6 grade-point average throughout high school and graduated with academic honors.

Improved the efficiency of 10 servers by redesigning the sidework setup so needed items were better organized and available at different locations in the restaurant.

Managed a yearbook staff of 15, and increased yearbook sales by 25% over the previous year while reducing costs through the use of on-campus computers for layouts and graphics.

Tailored accounting software for a small office, and trained three staff in its use, eliminating the need to hire an outside consultant.

Designed, wrote, and produced an off-campus newspaper funded entirely by advertising, featuring restaurants and coffee stores catering to teens, and a tutoring/study network of over 150 students.

Accomplishments comprise one of the most important parts of your resume, even if you list only two or three. Use the worksheet provided to develop descriptions of some of *your* accomplishments.

Experience summary: The experience summary lists positions you have held, including paid jobs, internships, apprenticeships, and volunteer work. Start with the most recent position and work backwards. Include your exact job title, name and address of employer/organization, and the beginning and ending dates that you of your employment (example: May, 2009 to January, 2010). Briefly list your duties and responsibilities, using as many *action* words as possible. If you have held several temporary jobs throughout your schooling, include those as well.

Education summary: The education summary is a list of the schools you have attended and the training programs you have completed, arranged in reverse order with the most recent experience at the top of the list. Include the name and location of the institution; the diploma, certificate, or degree earned; and the course emphasis. You may also include the year you graduated or the years you attended.

Optional sections: If you decide to include any of these sections, put them at or near the end of your resume.

• **Personal information.** Some people like to include a section entitled "Personal," which mentions health (always "excellent"), marital status, number of children, date of birth, hobbies, etc. Keep in mind that an employer by law cannot ask you about many of these things. The reason such laws exist is to protect you against discrimination based on age and other factors. Don't include this kind of information if you are concerned about possible discrimination.

• **Honors.** If you have received trophies, awards, scholarships, or other honors, you may list them.

• **Memberships.** List school and community organizations to which you belong, and charitable organizations for which you have volunteered.

• **Languages.** If you are fluent in any languages besides English, list them.

• **References:** If you are new to the job market and your resume is very brief, you might want to include three character references to lend credibility and fill space. Otherwise, type the references neatly on a separate sheet of paper, including complete names and addresses, and make copies. Provide a copy to any prospective employer who requests one.

Put Your Accomplishments into Words

One at a time, recall each work experience you have had. Ask yourself, "What did I do that made a positive difference in this situation?" Write down anything that comes to mind. Don't be concerned about wording; you can go back and create *action* statements later.

Next, one at a time, think about the different aspects of your school and community experience — projects, student organizations, special events, extracurricular activities, awards, contests or recitals, athletics, arts, service projects, etc. Again, each time you concentrate on a new area or time frame, ask yourself, "What positive difference did I make?" Did you:

...develop or implement a plan?

...resolve a problem or conflict?

...improve a procedure?

...build or repair something?

...win an award?

...earn a certificate, scholarship, or athletic letter?

...lead a group?

...chair a committee?

...plan a major event?

...raise money?

...contribute help to a cause or person

...master a difficult subject, course, or program?

Accomplishments

_____

_____

_____

_____

_____

_____

_____

_____

_____

_____

_____

_____

_____

_____

_____

_____

_____

_____

_____

_____

_____

_____

_____

_____

Sample Beginner Resume

Claudia Martin
333 High Hill Road
Hometown, State 12345
(111) 123-4567
cmartin@aol.com

Objective: Medical administrator in a hospital, clinic, or private practice.

Summary: Extremely capable in all aspects of medical administration, including scheduling and receiving patients, maintaining physician calendars, billing, insurance processing, and emergency procedures. Well organized, diligent, accurate, and energetic, with excellent human-relations skills.

Achievements: Helped to organize a community fund raiser benefiting a major health organization, which was attended by approximately 3,000 people and netted over $30,000.

Completed two medical internships in the period of time usually allotted for one, and received excellent evaluations at both.

Elected to student-government three years in a row, holding the offices of representative, secretary, and vice president.

Experience: Administrator-intern, Jan-April, 2010, Clark-Shelby Orthopedic Group, 999 Rockland Way, Hometown, State, Zip.

Administrator-intern, Jan-April, 2010, Centerview Children's Hospital, 1235 Center Street, Hometown, State, Zip.

Volunteer Visitor Guide, 2007-2009, Centerview Children's Hospital, 1235 Center Street, Hometown, State, Zip.

Education: • Bailey College of Medical Careers, Medical Administrator Course, Graduated June, 2010.
• Hometown High School, Hometown, State.
  High School Diploma, June 2008.

Organizations: • Member, State Association of Medical Secretaries, 2009-present.
• Member, Hometown Community Choir, 2006-present
• Volunteer, American Heart Association, 2007-present.

Sample Experienced Resume

Brian Andrews
9992 Barcelona Court
Hometown, State 12345
(111) 987-6543
bandrews@aol.com

Objective:	Copywriter for an advertising/marketing firm or in the marketing department of a major corporation.
Summary of Qualifications:	Two years of experience writing creative, humorous copy for print ads and radio and television commercials. Specialize in comedy dialog and jingles. Fast and prolific, with excellent writing skills and conceptual ability. Accustomed to meeting deadlines and working with creative teams.
Accomplishments:	Received Media Orchid Award for radio commercial that boosted sponsoring company's sales 30% in three months.
	Designed a multimedia sales presentation for a chain of home-decorating stores that drew the largest attendance in company history to the company's booth at sixteen home expos across the country.
	Wrote and published the 2009 Hometown County Fair theme song, which was selected from 50 entries.
	Helped to organize and found the first radio station at Hometown Community College, and served as its DJ for two years.
Experience:	Copywriter, Image Design Group, 467 Leeds Avenue, Hometown, Zip. Wrote copy for advertising in broadcasting and print media; designed multimedia sales presentations, training tools, and educational packages; wrote numerous jingles and theme songs; and participated in the development of comprehensive marketing plans.
	Feature writer, Hometown Gazette, Hometown Community College. Covered campus news and events, conducted interviews, and reviewed drama department productions. Published over 80 feature articles.
	Manager, Disk Jockey, Station KSYN, Hometown Community College. Co-founded and managed the station; secured the donation of hundreds of samples of recorded music; and assisted/supervised students in clerical, technical, and advertising sales positions. Hosted ongoing music and talk shows and trained other DJs.
Education:	Hometown High School, Hometown, State. High School Diploma, June 2006.
	Hometown Community College, Hometown, State Major courses of study: Journalism and Drama A.A. Degree, June 2008

Resume Worksheet

_____
(Name)

_____
(Address)

_____
(City, State, Zip)

_____
(Phone Number)

_____
(email address)

Objective: _____

_____

Summary: _____

_____

_____

Accomplishments: _____

_____

_____

_____

_____

Experience: _____

_____

_____

_____

_____

Education: _____

_____

_____

Sample Letter of Introduction

August 4, 2010

Dr. Juanita Contreras, Administrator
Hilltop Medical Center
1000 South 15th Street
Bigcity, State 87654

Dear Dr. Contreras,

I recently graduated from Bailey College of Medical Careers in Hometown, with a certificate in Medical Administration, and am very interested in learning more about the employment opportunities at Hilltop Medical Center.

As my resume shows, I completed two 4-month internships, one at a large children's hospital and the other with a group of orthopedic physicians. In addition, I worked for two years as a volunteer at the same children's hospital, helping visitors find their way around and locate needed services. All of these experiences were very successful, and I am looking forward to securing a full-time position in the medical field.

I would like to spend twenty minutes with you, to find out more about your organization and to hear any ideas or advice you can give me. I will call your office within the next few days to schedule an appointment.

Thank you for your time and consideration.

Sincerely,

Claudia Martin
333 High Hill Road
Hometown, State 12345
(111) 123-4567
cmartin@aol.com

Sample Want-Ad Response

July 24, 2010

Director of Human Resources
The Milligan Group
3987 Enterprise Way
Anytown, State 12396

Dear Director:

I am writing in response to your advertisement in the July 19 issue of the Hometown Tribune for an experienced Advertising Copywriter.

I have spent two successful years writing copy for print ads and radio and television commercials. In particular, I have earned a bit of a reputation among clients and colleagues for my whimsical, memorable jingles. I have also helped to develop multimedia education, training, and sales presentations.

I am currently seeking new challenges and the opportunity to work with technology and a wide range of clients and creative professionals. Judging from my research, the Milligan Group would be ideal.

I have enclosed my resume, and will clear my schedule for an interview at your convenience. I look forward to hearing from you soon.

Sincerely

Brian Andrews
9992 Barcelona Court
Hometown, State 12345
(111) 987-6543
bandrews@aol.com

Ensuring Successful Interviews

Target:

The activities in this section will help you:

⇨ know what to expect during an interview.

⇨ prepare yourself through research and practice.

⇨ answer a wide range of typical interview questions.

⇨ gain valuable learnings from each interview, no matter what the outcome.

⇨ follow-up with winning thank-you notes.

It's Your Interview, Too

The interview is the toughest part of your job search, but it is also your greatest opportunity. Up until now, the employer has seen your information through your resume, cover letter, and application. Now, suddenly, you are much more than words on a page. You're a person.

You will probably feel nervous. That's okay. Interviewers expect you be to a little nervous; you wouldn't be normal if you weren't. Try to think of the interview as a two-way street — an exchange of information. You want to know more about the company and the company wants to know more about you. Specifically, the company wants to know what kind of person you are and what you can do for the organization.

Believe it or not, if you're prepared for the interview and concentrate on the organization and the person with whom you are talking (rather than on your fear), you'll quickly lose your nervousness and begin to demonstrate what every interviewer wants to see:

- confidence in yourself
- interest in the company
- enthusiasm about work
- self-respect (a preview of good character)

Before the Interview

Prepare for the interview. Don't go in completely cold. Know something about the company as well as the specific job you've applied for. Review your qualifications and resume. Be prepared to answer a broad range of questions.

Research. Find out as much as you can about the company. Pay an advance visit and request a copy of any available printed materials: brochures, annual reports, catalogs, etc. If possible, talk with someone who already works for the company. Use the internet and study the company website. Locate and read any articles or other information about the company.

Jot down questions you have about the company as a result of your research. List major facts about the company, too. Commit all of this to memory so that you can mentally refer to it during the interview.

Practice. One way to prepare for the interview is to role play. Ask your counselor, a friend, or parent to play the part of the interviewer and ask you questions similar to those that might be asked during the interview. Use the "Sample Interview Questions" as a guide

Another way to practice is to do lots of interviewing. Use interviews to get information and referrals as well as to land a job. Prioritize your job prospects and interview with the ones you care *least* about first. Save the ones you want most until *last*. By then you'll be an experienced interviewer.

Dress appropriately. Be well groomed. No matter what the job or how you think people at this company dress on a day-to-day basis, wear businesslike attire to your interview — suit or tailored dress, simple natural hairstyle, conservative jewelry, and light makeup. No gum, no smoking, no strong perfume or after shave, no garlic or onions.

Be organized. You may be asked to complete a standard employment application prior to your interview, so take all the information (social security number, driver's license, names, addresses, dates, etc.) you might need to accurately answer questions about your schooling, employment history and references. In addition, take a notepad and pencil, extra resumes, and your references on a separate sheet.

Arrive early and alone. Give yourself plenty of time to deal with traffic delays, weather conditions, and finding the location. Upon arriving, greet the receptionist pleasantly. Then use any extra time to relax, take a few deep breathes, compose yourself, and look over your notes.

Sample Interview Questions

Here is a list of typical interview questions. Duplicate the sheet and write in your answers prior to each interview. Give the same questions to your role-play partner.

Tell me a little about yourself. _____

_____

_____

Why do you want this job? _____

_____

_____

What would you like to know about this company? _____

_____

_____

Where do you want to be five years from now? _____

_____

_____

What are your career goals? _____

_____

_____

What were your best subjects in school? _____

_____

_____

What have you studied in school that will help you do this job? _____

_____

_____

_____

Why should we hire you? _____

_____

_____

Why did you leave your last job? _____

_____

_____

What makes you a good worker? _____

_____

_____

What are your strengths/weaknesses? _____

_____

_____

What can you do for this company? _____

_____

_____

What do you expect this company to do for you? _____

_____

_____

What do you know about this company? _____

_____

_____

If you had a conflict with one of your coworkers, how would you handle it? _____

_____

_____

_____

_____

During the Interview

Look alive. Stand tall, shake hands firmly, make eye contact with each person you meet, and smile. When you are introduced to someone, repeat his or her name aloud immediately. This will help you remember it. Don't sit down until invited to do so.

Listen. Generally speaking, interviewers like nothing better than to talk about the company, the company's goals, plans, and accomplishments, and how the job for which you have applied fits within this picture. Look attentive, maintain eye contact, show genuine interest, and use your active-listening skills.

Ask questions. As the interviewer talks, some of the questions you developed while researching the company will come to mind along with more questions triggered by the interviewer's statements. Ask them. Questions prove that you are listening and that you've done your homework.

Answer questions. When the interviewer asks you a question, answer briefly (2 minutes maximum) and specifically. If the answer is a simple "yes" or "no," try to add a little information. For example, if asked, "Do you think you'll enjoy selling?" say something like, "Yes, I've always liked meeting people and assisting them. I think I'll do very well."

Some questions are illegal in a pre-employment interview. If you are asked questions about your age, marital status, number of children, use of birth control, plans to have children, religious beliefs, citizenship, birthplace, criminal record, club membership, family or financial situation, or medical condition, you do not have to answer. Rather than simply refusing to answer, which might annoy or embarrass the interviewer, try to sidestep the question by saying pleasantly, "I'm not sure what that has to do with this job. Can you help me out here?"

Be positive. Show that you are confident of your ability to do the job. Don't talk about problems, worries, doubts, or weaknesses. If the interviewer asks what your greatest weakness is (interviewers often do), cheerfully sidestep the issue by saying something like, "Right now I can't think of any" or "Well, sometimes I get so busy that I forget to walk my dog."

Don't discuss salary. All the experts seem to agree on this one. Don't talk about money until you've been offered the job. If your interviewer wants to talk about it, just listen and nod.

After the Interview

Record your reactions. Take a few minutes while the interview is fresh in your mind. Write down your impressions of the company, and how you think the interview went. What were your strengths during the interview? What mistakes did you make? What do you need to work on? Duplicate and use the "Interview Reaction Form".

Send a thank-you note. Within 24 hours of the interview, write a short note to your interviewer, expressing your appreciation for the opportunity, the time, and all the helpful information you gained. If possible, refer to something specific that occurred during the interview. Finally, restate your interest in the job and your confidence that you can do the job. If you had more than one interviewer, send a separate note to each one. This note can be hand written or be included in an email.

Get information. If you are not offered the job, take a few minutes to find out why. Call the interviewer and ask for feedback. Tell him or her that you would like to know what you can do better in the future. Be positive. Don't complain. Listen and learn.

Interview Reaction Form

Interview Date: _____ Contact Phone # _____

Name of Company: _____

Position Sought: _____

Name of Interviewer: _____
Title

Email: _____

High Points: _____

_____

_____

_____

_____

Low Points: _____

_____

_____

_____

_____

Things to Remember Next Time: _____

_____

_____

_____

_____

Follow Up/Additional Notes: _____

_____

_____

Thank-you note sent to: _____
Date

Sample Thank-you Note

October 20, 2010

Mr. James Smythe
Personnel Director
XYZ Company
789 E. 10th Street
Newcity, State 12345

Dear Mr. Smythe,

I appreciate the time you took to interview me last Wednesday for the contract administrator opening at XYZ Company. It's exactly the kind of position I am seeking.

Your company is doing some very exciting work in the business software field and I would like to be involved in the process. I believe that my experience handling contracts at two other companies and my knowledge of computers makes me especially well qualified for the job.

I am looking forward to hearing from you and to joining your organization.

Sincerely,

Maria Lopez
123 Your Street
Hometown, State 12359
jsmythe@aol.com

Job Keeping Skills

Developing and Maintaining a Positive Attitude

What Is Attitude?

Here are some expressions you've probably heard (or used):

"She has a bad attitude."
"I don't like your attitude."
"You'd better change your attitude."
"She has a great attitude."
"His biggest problem is his attitude."
"What is your attitude about this?"

An attitude is a mental position or posture. It's the way you're leaning *inside*. And just like physical posture, attitude is affected by your thoughts and feelings. Since you have different feelings and thoughts about different things, you probably have many different attitudes, too. For example, your attitude toward studying may be quite different from your attitude toward working. Or your attitude about computer class may be very different from your attitude toward history class.

Recalling Attitudes

Even though attitudes are inside, they usually show. That's because we express our attitudes by the things we say and do. We express them through our words and our faces. They show in our energy level and in the choices we make.

Think of a time when you *strongly disliked* a person's attitude. See if you can describe how that person came across. You might get some ideas by looking at the list of words, at the bottom of the page.

_____

_____

_____

_____

Now, think of a time when you *liked* or *admired* a person's attitude. Again, see if any words on the list below describe how the person came across.

_____

_____

_____

_____

arrogant	confident	afraid	bossy
sullen	interested	wimpy	critical
angry	kind	cheerful	reluctant
argumentative	responsible	eager	complaining
defensive	helpful	adventurous	careless
bored	humble	industrious	whiny

Carry-over Attitudes

Everyone has days when things go wrong. Your parent yells at you. You have a fight with your boyfriend or girlfriend. You lose your brand new jacket. A problem in your family or a bad grade on a test causes you to get upset. You feel frustrated or sad — or perhaps you walk around all day carrying a mixed load of guilt and anger. Then you go to work. What is likely to happen?

Think of a time when you carried a bad attitude from one place to another.

What caused the bad attitude?

_____

_____

How did you express this attitude?

_____

_____

If you got grease on your hands from working on your car, or if you got dirt on your hands from pulling weeds, you'd wash it off before going to your job. You wouldn't want the grease or the dirt to get on the things you touch at work — the computer, cash register, clothing, food, etc.

Take the same precaution with your attitude. Clean it up before you go to work. Don't let your frustration, sadness, guilt, or anger touch your employer, coworkers, or customers. Don't make other people suffer because you're having a bad day. This goes for other areas of your life as well – school, home teams, etc.

Carry over positive attitudes ONLY!

Assessing Your Attitude

Your attitude is an expression of your thoughts and feelings. Your parents, teachers and friends will probably think you have a good attitude if you are eager to try new tasks, work hard without supervision, stick with hard tasks, are cheerful, friendly, accept responsibility, and obey rules.

What was your attitude today?

_____

_____

_____

How did you show your attitude?

_____

_____

_____

Pay attention to the attitudes of others around you. When someone's attitude really stands out — whether good or bad — write down what you see. (Be subtle. Don't stare, and do the writing later.)

Type of Attitude	How Expressed	Effects of Attitude

How to Maintain A Positive Attitude

Focusing on the positive can help you maintain a positive attitude. Here are some important things to remember when you're working:

✔ Be enthusiastic. Show that you appreciate being in your job.

✔ Treat every person you meet as though he or she is the most important person you'll meet all day. If this feels awkward at first, do it anyway. Pretty soon, people will become truly important to you, and the awkwardness will go away.

✔ Develop a strong handshake. Then, while you're shaking hands, think a positive thought. For example: "This seems like a person I could learn a lot from. I'd really like to know this person better."

✔ Act like someone who gets the job done. Don't say, "I'll try." It sounds uncertain. Instead say, "I will" or "I'll have an answer for you by five." (Then make sure that you do!)

✔ Be *for* things, not *against* things. For example, be *for* a meeting on Tuesday, rather than *against* a meeting on Monday. Do you see the difference? Here's another example: Be *for* designing a new window display, rather than *tired of* (against) the one that's in the window now. Be *for* a new billing software, rather than *sick of* (against) the current one. In other words, avoid complaining. When you state what you are for, you focus on positive solutions.

✔ Focus on the parts of the job that you like. There are bound to be things you don't like about your job. If you think about them all the time, you develop a negative attitude. How can you do your best if you only see the worst? Focus on the positive parts of your job. Work to change the negative parts. If they can't be changed, accept them.

Attitude Inventory

Being able to develop a positive attitude is one of the most important skills there is because it enriches all parts of life from school to work, every relationship, and all activities. For some people a positive attitude comes easily. For others it is hard work to do so. It also seems to be that attitude is contagious. When you're around positive people, you tend to be more positive too. Take an inventory of your attitude as it relates to important aspects of your life. Think about school, friendships, teams, clubs, and family life. If you have a job, think about that too.

List the things you like and dislike in different areas of your life. Then fill in the columns with your current behaviors (How I Show It) and your ideas about future behaviors (How to Change It, or How to Live with It).

Likes	How I Show It	How to Change It	How to Live with It
Dislikes			

Taking Charge of Your Appearance

Target:

The activities in this section will help you:

⇨ determine what is appropriate attire for different types of jobs.

⇨ identify the main aspects of good grooming.

⇨ plan the changes you need to make in your appearance.

Does Appearance Really Count?

Absolutely! In many types of jobs, its okay to dress casually and comfortably. In others, professional looking business attire is required. In still others, the employer provides a uniform. But regardless of whether you wear a suit or jeans, you must be clean, combed, and well groomed.

Appearance is especially important if your job puts you in contact with the public. If you're the person behind the register or the counter, to customers *you* represent the company. If customers feel satisfied with the impression you make and the service you give, they'll probably come back. If your appearance or manner turns them off, they might take their business to a different company.

What Do the Ads Show?

Go to the magazine section of a supermarket or bookstore. Study the advertising in several business magazines. Choose magazines about economics and finance, management, computers, and other topics that are important to business owners. The companies that advertise in these magazines are hoping to sell their products to businesses, so the ads are designed to appeal to business people. Look at three or more different types of magazines.

1. Describe how the models in several ads were dressed.

_____

_____

_____

2. What did you notice about hair?

_____

_____

_____

3. What about makeup and jewelry?

_____

_____

_____

4. What kinds of shoes did you see?

_____

_____

_____

There's More to Grooming Than Meets the Eye

Some things about grooming can't be seen, but they *can* be smelled. Take care to be as pleasing to the nostrils as you are to the eyes.

• **Check your breath.** People with bad breath often don't have a clue. If you visit your dentist and brush and floss regularly, you probably have nothing to worry about. However, if you're not sure, by all means <u>ask someone</u>.

• **Shower and apply deodorant daily.** Your body chemistry is unique, so find a soap and a deodorant that are effective for you. Experiment with shampoos, too.

• **Go easy on perfumes and aftershave.** No matter how pleasing the scent to you, some customers and coworkers are sure to dislike it. Other people may be allergic to it. Don't be the cause of headaches and wheezing!

Assessing Your Own Appearance

Look at yourself. Based on your observations, what changes do you need to make in order to be appropriately groomed for a job? Be honest!

	Present Condition	Ideal Condition	Steps to Take	Target Date
HAIR				
FACE				
TEETH				
HANDS & NAILS				
CLOTHING				

What Would You Wear to Work?

It's important to be well groomed and dressed appropriately for the type of job you are doing. It sends a clear message that you want to please your employer and customers, that you have respect for them, and that your high personal standards will transfer to your work.

Below is a list of several different jobs. Pick at least two in which you might have interest. Think carefully about the "statement" you want to make to your employer and customers, and then, in the space provided below, write a detailed description of what you would wear to work.

- Secretary
- Auto repair specialist
- Insurance salesperson
- Server in an upscale restaurant
- Day care center teacher
- Grocery store clerk
- Minister
- Retail store owner
- Shoe salesperson
- Dentist
- Hairdresser
- Bus driver
- Recreation center coach
- Travel agent

_____

_____

_____

_____

_____

_____

_____

_____

Being There: The First Requirement

Target:

The activities in this section will help you:

⇨ recognize how attendance and punctuality affect coworkers, productivity, and your job goals.

⇨ differentiate between acceptable and unacceptable work absences.

⇨ properly call in a work absence.

⇨ assess your own punctuality and attendance habits.

The Trouble with Cherie

More often than not, Cherie slipped into her work station a few minutes late. Maybe two minutes, maybe ten. That wouldn't have been too bad, except that a couple of times a week she left work a half hour or so early. On her way out the door, she'd call something over her shoulder about an appointment, or picking up her brother, or the line at the bank. Her coworkers would just look at each other. Lunch "hours" were the worst — they never lasted less than ninety minutes. Cherie liked to point out that she often worked late and took work home over the weekends, so the company owed her the extra time. (No one *else* could remember seeing any evidence of this additional effort.)

Cherie's absences were higher than other employees, too. Sometimes she didn't get around to calling in sick until a couple of hours into her shift, when everyone had already spent half the morning trying to cover her work as well as their own.

When Cherie was fired, it didn't surprise anyone. None of her coworkers phoned to express their sympathy because, frankly, they didn't have any. Cherie had lost the respect of her supervisor and coworkers alike.

What was Cherie's attitude toward her time at work?

_____

_____

How do habits of arriving late, leaving early, and taking long lunch breaks get started?

_____

_____

How Is Your Attendance Now?

Behavior patterns (habits) frequently carry over from one setting to another. Think about your attendance at school, club meetings, athletic practices, and other regular events. Do you see any patterns that need changing?

How many days of school do you usually miss each month? _____

What are the most frequent causes of your absences? _____

Do you think most employers would accept these as good reasons to stay home from work? Why or why not?

_____

An Ounce of Prevention

What do athletes do to avoid missing games? They stay in shape so they'll be less apt to get sick or injured. What do actors do to avoid missing performances? They keep their bodies in top condition and get plenty of rest. What do *you* do when an important event is coming up and the last thing in the world you want is to get sick and miss it? You probably make an extra effort to take care of yourself. For example, perhaps you:

✔ eat right
✔ get plenty of sleep
✔ take vitamins
✔ exercise
✔ when exposed to illness, wash your hands frequently

Treat work like a special event. Prevent absences by taking care of yourself!

To Work or Not to Work

Go down this list and check (✔) all the items that you think are acceptable reasons for being absent from work:

Cause of Absence	Employer Reaction
___ headache	_____
___ don't feel like going	_____
___ cold	_____
___ shopping	_____
___ baby-sitting	_____
___ doctor's appointment	_____
___ homework	_____
___ allergies	_____
___ sprained ankle	_____
___ flu	_____
___ upset stomach	_____
___ cramps	_____
___ no sleep the previous night	_____

Now, pretend that you are an employer. Go back and circle any of the checked items that you (in your employer role) disagree with. On the lines to the right, explain the employer's point of view.

What is the one situation that will cause you to miss the most work?

_____

How can you prevent this from happening?

_____

_____

_____

_____

_____

How to Call in An Absence

When you have a job, and you have a valid reason for missing work, always call your employer as soon as you know you will not be at work, no matter what the reason. Your employer may decide to find a substitute for you. When you don't call, your job doesn't get done. This not only makes your supervisor unhappy, it places an unfair burden on your coworkers.

Before you pick up the phone, take a minute to think about the work that you would normally be doing on the day you must be absent. Is any critical task going to be neglected because of your absence? An important order? A phone call? Be ready to tell your supervisor about such critical tasks so that other people can be asked to do them. Here are some additional suggestions:

1. Follow your company's guidelines for reporting absences.
2. Give as much notice as you can. Talk to your supervisor as soon as you know you are going to be absent.
3. Speak clearly and precisely.
4. Say that you will not be able to come to work. Be specific about the day and date.
5. Give a brief reason why you will not be in. Be honest.
6. Mention any tasks or assignments that cannot be postponed until you return to work. Let your supervisor know that these will have to be completed by someone else.
7. If possible, suggest a coworker who could take charge of these tasks.
8. State when you expect to be back at work.
9. Apologize for any inconvenience your absence may cause.
10. Inform your supervisor at once if your return date changes.

Becoming a Skillful Communicator

Target

The activities in this section will help you:

⇨ become a more effective listener and speaker.

⇨ improve voice quality and nonverbal skills.

⇨ identify patterns of communication in your job setting.

⇨ improve phone skills.

⇨ evaluate your communication skills.

Learning to Listen

Though most of us have received formal training in reading, writing, and speaking, few of us have been taught to listen. Why? Probably because we take listening for granted. We assume that there's basically nothing to it — we just sit there while the other person talks.

Not true. Listening is a complex process. First of all, it involves language, which is like a code. As a listener, you have to *decode* every word to get its meaning. This involves complicated mental processes — interpreting, evaluating, comparing to past experiences, arriving at conclusions, and making inferences, to name a few. Then you have to take what you *think* you've heard and use it as the basis for formulating a response, which involves *encoding* (choosing the right word to say). At this point the process reverses and starts all over again, with you as the speaker.

Truly good listeners are pretty hard to find. That's why the ability to listen effectively is going to play an important role in your success — at school, on the job, and in your personal life.

How to Recognize a Good Listener

Listed below are characteristics of a good listener. Check ones that describe you most of the time.

A good listener:

___ Faces the speaker.

___ Looks into the speaker's eyes, but doesn't stare.

___ Is relaxed, but attentive.

___ Keeps an open mind.

___ Listens to the words and tries to understand what the speaker is saying.

___ Doesn't interrupt or fidget.

___ Waits for the speaker to pause to ask clarifying questions.

___ Asks questions only to ensure understanding of something that has been said (avoiding questions that disrupt the speaker's train of thought).

___ Tries to feel what the speaker is feeling (shows empathy).

___ Nods and says "uh huh," or summarizes to let the speaker know he or she is listening.

___ Pays attention to what *isn't* said — to feelings, facial expressions, gestures, posture, and other nonverbal cues.

What is your strongest quality as a listener? _____

_____

What is your weakest quality as a listener? _____

_____

How can you become a better listener? _____

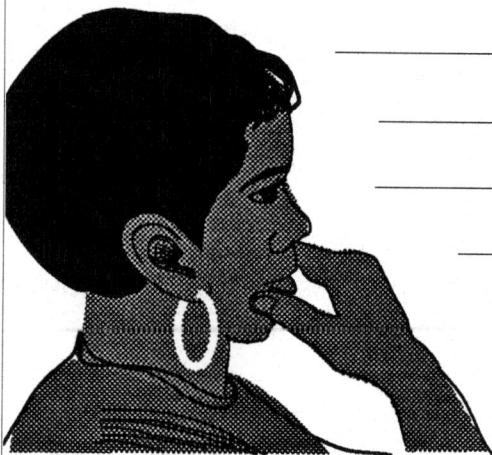

_____

_____

_____

_____

_____

_____

_____

How to Give "Active Listening" Feedback

The difference between active listening and passive listening is in the listener's level of involvement. As a passive listener, you just listen, nothing more. As an active listener, you say and do things to *let the speaker know* that you are listening and understanding what is being said. Besides nodding and saying, "uh huh," you can:

• Summarize.
You're saying that you might have to change everyone's schedule next week because three workers will be on vacation.

If I understand you correctly, you want to return this item for cash, and exchange these other two items for a different size.

• Restate feelings.
You must be feeling pretty frustrated.

You sound really pleased!

You're worried that we might not get the job finished.

Closing such a big sale makes you feel proud.

More Listening Tips

✔ Mentally screen out distractions, like background activity and noise. In addition, try not to focus on the speaker's accent or speech mannerisms to the point where they become distractions. Finally, don't be distracted by your own thoughts, feelings, or biases.

✔ When listening for long stretches, focus on (and remember) key words. Key words usually show <u>action</u> or <u>feeling</u>.

✔ When dealing with difficult coworkers or customers, spend more time listening than speaking.

✔ When in doubt about whether to listen or speak, it's best to keep listening.

How Do You Sound?

✔ Is your voice clear, steady, and confident?

✔ Does your voice show enthusiasm and energy?

✔ Do you keep your pitch at a pleasant medium level?

✔ Do you sound direct and straightforward, as though you mean what you say?

✔ Do you tone down the volume of your voice when you're tempted to speak too loudly?

✔ Do you eliminate "uhs" and "ahs" when suggesting ideas or courses of action?

✔ Do you make a conscious effort to break annoying verbal habits such as the use of "like" and "you know."

Sounding Better Six Ways

1. Pay attention to your **tone** of voice. Tone conveys feeling.

2. Pronounce words **clearly**. Don't slur or mumble.

3. Keep your **pitch** at a medium level.

4. Use appropriate **volume**. People shouldn't have to strain to hear you, but they shouldn't need earplugs either.

5. Project **energy** and **enthusiasm**.

6. Control your **pace**. Don't race and don't idle. Cruise.

Avoid Muddy Messages:

Do you ever feel totally confused trying to have a conversation with a person who...
...can't seem to finish a sentence?

...starts to express one thought and, right in the middle of the sentence, jumps to a completely different thought?

...makes such vague statements that you can't get any real meaning from them?

...keeps going on and on without stopping until you finally get too tired to listen at all?

Don't make these mistakes yourself. Speak in complete sentences. (You don't have to make them fancy, just finish them.) Don't jump from topic to topic. When you speak, try to paint a picture in the mind of the listener. Choose descriptive words and make the picture as vivid and complete as possible, in as few words as possible. Don't dominate. Stop talking occasionally and give your listener a chance to respond.

Piling on the Pronouns

One of the most common culprits in vague, muddy communication is the pronoun. A pronoun —which acts as a substitute for a noun — is a very useful part of speech, except when overused.

Mr. Jones is sick. He won't be coming in today. That's easy to understand. "He" is Mr. Jones.

But what about this:

I don't know what happened regarding that matter. I'll ask him what he thinks about the way it was done. In the meantime, we should put this other issue on hold until we have an answer to these questions.

In order to understand that statement, the listener must be able to mentally answer these questions:

1. What is "that matter?"
2. Why is "what happened" concerning that matter important?
3. Who is "him?"
4. What is "it" and how *was* it done?
5. What is the "other issue?"
6. What are the "other questions?"

Be specific. Use complete and correct terms. Don't substitute a pronoun (he, she, it, they, them) unless there is no doubt about the subject to which you are referring.

Words Are Only Part of It

What you say *without* words — by the way you look, stand, and move — sends messages that sometimes convey more meaning (or a different meaning) than your words. To communicate effectively, your nonverbal actions and expressions must match your verbal messages.

Try to identify any negative nonverbal habits you may have. Then work on changing them. Answer these questions:

- How often do your facial expressions show dissatisfaction? boredom? resentment? doubt?
- Is your voice frequently whiny? shrill? angry? sarcastic?
- How do you handle eye contact? Do you avoid looking into people's eyes? Do you stare until people look away?
- What about body movements? Do you usually stand straight or do you slouch down? Do you look relaxed and open or tense and ready for a fight?

Remember that different cultures attach different meanings to nonverbal behaviors. If you are working with or for someone from a different cultural background, try to find out the meaning of certain actions in that person's culture. For example, in some Asian cultures, people show respect by lowering their eyes. Pointing with the index finger is considered insulting in some cultures.

Communicating on the Telephone

The main difference between communicating on the phone and talking with someone in person is that the sound of your voice — pitch, tone, volume, speed, clarity, energy and enthusiasm — becomes even more important than it is face-to-face. Since, of the five senses, only hearing is being utilized during a phone conversation, all cues related to that sense are intensified in importance.

Think about your own experience using the phone and answer these questions.

1. Have you ever talked on the phone to someone whose voice sounded flat or dull? What were your thoughts and feelings?

_____

_____

_____

_____

_____

2. Have you ever tried to have a phone conversation with a person who was constantly interrupted by other calls or by people in the background? What was your reaction?

_____

_____

_____

_____

3. Have you ever tried to explain something over the phone to a person who didn't seem to be listening? How did you feel and what did you do?

_____

_____

_____

_____

_____

4. Have you ever tried to get information over the phone from a person who seemed unable to finish a sentence or speak understandably? How did you handle the situation?

_____

_____

_____

_____

Phone-Voice Checklist

How well do you demonstrate these positive phone skills?

▼ Convey alertness and interest.

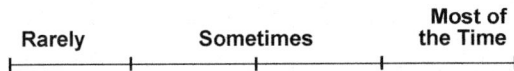

Rarely	Sometimes	Most of the Time

▼ Speak with a "smile" in your voice.

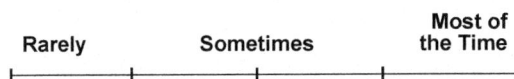

Rarely	Sometimes	Most of the Time

▼ Use simple, straightforward language.

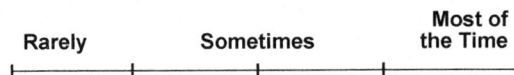

Rarely	Sometimes	Most of the Time

▼ Speak clearly and distinctly.

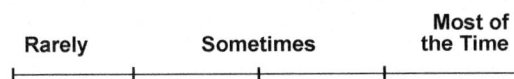

Rarely	Sometimes	Most of the Time

▼ Speak in a normal tone at moderate speed.

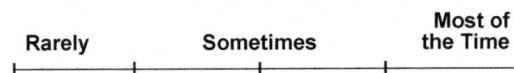

Rarely	Sometimes	Most of the Time

Tips for Using the Phone Properly at work

When you make a call:

1. Collect your thoughts. Know the purpose of your call and approximately what you are going to say.
2. Take notes. Always have paper and pencil at hand.
3. Immediately state your name and the name of the company.
4. Offer a pleasant greeting.
5. Ask if the person has time to talk.
6. Explain why you are calling.
7. Allow time for reactions.
8. Be ready to answer questions.
9. Don't put people on hold.
10. Express your appreciation before hanging up.

When you receive a call:

1. Give your name along with a greeting. "Good morning. Esther speaking."
2. Take notes — or be ready to.
3. Ask, "How may I help you?" and get right to business.
4. Before transferring a call, explain to the caller who will be picking up the line.
5. Avoid putting people on hold for more than a few seconds.

Your Communication Skills

Take your time to think about your skills as a communicator. Be as honest as you can in assessing yourself when you answer these questions.

1. How's your judgment? Do you know when to listen, when to talk, and when to wait for a better time?

    Always   Sometimes   Never

2. Do you come across to others as honest and sincere?

    Always   Sometimes   Never

3. Do you listen "actively," giving the speaker all of your attention?

    Always   Sometimes   Never

4. Do you speak clearly, and convey information completely and accurately?

    Always   Sometimes   Never

5. What is the overall effect you think you have on others when you speak to them?

    Positive   Neutral   Negative

6. On what occasions have you communicated particularly well verbally, and why do you think things went so well those times?

_____

_____

7. When have you "goofed," and what were the reasons for it?

_____

_____

8. What do you do when other people ignore or dismiss what you say?

_____

9. Choose one area of communication at a time to focus on and improve.

___ Active listening   ___ Speaking ability
___ Nonverbal communication (body language)   ___ Telephone skills
___ Voice quality.   ___ Breaking a bad speech habit.

Describe the specific improvement you're after (your goal) and how you plan to achieve it?

_____

_____

_____

_____

Following Directions with Care

Target:

The activities in this section will help you:

▷ clarify directions through listening and questioning.

▷ learn to receive directions completely and accurately.

▷ think through directions before acting on them.

Listen and Question!

When you were a kid, do you remember frequently asking "Why?" when adults gave you directions? Children are naturally curious. They want to understand how the world works and why things have to be done in certain ways.

In growing up, you may have lost some of that persistent desire to understand. You may have concluded that people are more interested in having you do what you're told than they are in helping you understand why. Well, if your curiosity has become a little dulled, now's the time to sharpen it up!

When people give you directions, pay close attention. Don't be hesitant or shy about asking questions. As you listen, encourage yourself to be curious and inquiring. In order to follow directions thoughtfully and carefully, you've got to comprehend them. You must know exactly what is expected of you. Listening and questioning are two of the most important skills you can use.

Grab a Pen and Listen!

✔ The first and most important thing to do when someone starts giving instructions or directions is to *listen*. Not with part of your attention, but with all of your attention. Not while doing something else, but without distractions.

✔ Take notes while receiving directions. Keep them very brief — if you get too involved in writing, you won't be listening.

✔ When the person is finished giving directions, go over your notes and make sure you understand them. Skim through the entire set of directions to get an overview and to check your mental image of the task. If you have a question or don't understand something, ask for clarification as soon as possible.

✔ Summarize to confirm your understanding. If at all possible, restate the directions (or read them back). For example, you might say:

*Let me see if I got this right.
You want me to...*

The way you want me to do this is to...

Briefly restated, the steps are:
- **Listen**
- **Take Notes**
- **Ask questions**
- **Summarize**

What Went Wrong?

All of us get directions mixed up sometimes. We assemble an item the wrong way so the pieces don't fit. We show up at the wrong time or in the wrong place to meet a friend. We read the wrong chapter or write a report using the wrong format. We get lost on the way to a destination, even though we wrote down the directions.

Think of a time when you bungled an assignment or commitment by failing to follow directions. Try to recall exactly what you were trying to accomplish and as much as possible about the directions. Now, analyze your mistake. What could you have done better as you received and followed the directions?

Listening. I could have... _____

_____

_____

Taking notes. I could have... _____

_____

Asking questions. I could have asked...

_____

_____

Summarizing. I could have said... _____

_____

_____

_____

_____

Take a Moment to Think It Through

The next time someone gives you instructions whether it's at school, at home, or on your job, take a few minutes to answer these questions:

What is the purpose of these directions or instructions?

_____

_____

What kind of prior knowledge is needed to carry out these instructions?

_____

_____

What equipment and/or materials are required?

_____

_____

What questions would I like answers to before I follow these instructions?

_____

_____

_____

_____

Where can I go for answers to these questions?

_____

_____

_____

_____

_____

Build a Sequence of Steps

Following instructions involves sequencing — doing things in order. Sometimes your teacher or supervisor at work will give a direction that just describes the end product. For example a work assignment might be:

Redo the gift-wrap display before you leave today.

For school you may need to complete a research paper by the end of the week. How do you sequence these things?

When you need to complete important tasks, for the best, most effective results, you can construct a sequence of steps. In order to do that you must figure out what the steps are, and put those steps in the proper (or best) order.

As you clarify each step, questions will come to mind that must be answered before the step can be completed. Jot those down as you think of them.

Sequencing Matrix

Use this matrix as a guide the next time you decide to sequence a set of instructions. (Use it to sequence printed directions from guides and manuals, too.)

Summary of Instructions/Directions: _____

_____

STEP	QUESTIONS
1._____	_____
	_____
2._____	_____
	_____
3._____	_____
	_____
4._____	_____
	_____
5._____	_____
	_____

Managing Time and Being Productive

Make and Cut a "Day Pie"

A good way to begin gaining better control of your time is to find out how you are using it now. One way to do this is to keep a time log for a week or two. Write down exactly what you do with every half-hour of your time, twenty-four hours a day. A faster (though less accurate) way is to estimate the amount of time you spend involved in major types of activities. A "day pie" is a simple method to use.

Take a blank sheet of paper and draw a circle to fill the space. This is your pie. Next, estimate how many hours or parts of hours you spend in school, at work, eating, watching TV, playing a game, reading, texting, talking on the phone, and engaging in other categories of activities. Show each portion of time as a slice of the pie; then label each slice. When you are finished, study the results. Ask yourself:

• What categories seem to be getting too much or too little time? What can I do about them?

• Are any activities completely missing from my day that I would like to add on a regular basis? What are they and how can I fit them in?

Use a Daily Planner

Planners come in hundreds of different sizes and designs. They can be purchased, downloaded, or you can even create your own. All planners contain a calendar and most have sections for recording notes, goals, daily tasks, phone numbers, and email addresses. The purpose of a planner is to help you organize your activities, which in turn enables you control your time.

Consistent use of a planning system can give a huge boost to your personal productivity. Your planner doesn't have to be a big, bulky three-ring binder; it can fit neatly in your pocket or purse. In addition to a calendar, just make sure it includes places for:
• listing each day's tasks
• recording notes
• writing goals

Prioritize Your Activities

Get in the habit of writing down everything that you want to accomplish each day. Some people like to start their list the night before, then finalize it in the morning. Others make it their first task of the day. Write down everything from small, optional errands to the big, essential tasks. Then go back and indicate the importance of each item by giving it an:

A = must be done
B = should be done (but possibly could wait a day or so)
C = could be done (nice, but not necessary)

Next, give the A's a logical numbered sequence (A-1, A-2, A-3, etc.). The most important A might be a meeting with your supervisor. However, because the meeting is scheduled for 3:00 p.m., it will not be A-1 on your list. That's because you have several hours in which to accomplish other A's (and maybe some B's) before that meeting. Finally, number the B's. The C's don't require numbering.

This process gives you a crystal clear picture of what you are going to do with your time. Complete the A's first. **Your goal is to accomplish every A on the list — which is also the definition of a successful day!**

Be Guided by Your Goals

A goal is a target, a destination, something to shoot for. Goals can center on having something — clothes, a car, money — or they can center on achieving — finishing school, going to college, having a career, becoming famous, gaining knowledge and honors.

Goals provide direction and purpose in life. They also give you a foolproof way of judging the importance of your activities. All you have to do is ask, "How does this activity help me reach one of my goals?" If an answer doesn't pop right into your head, you can probably give that activity a low priority.

How to Write A Goal

A Goal is...

✔ **Specific**

Vivid, descriptive, detailed wording gives a goal real power.

✔ **Realistic**

You might have to work hard for it, but it's definitely reachable.

✔ **Stated in positive language**

"Have a neat, organized, pleasant bedroom" is better than "Get rid of junk".

✔ **Measurable, with a target date**

"Be a lean 175 pounds by June 15" is much better than "Lose weight now."

✔ **Written**

When you write a goal, it has more importance, and since you can "see" your goal, often it is a good reminder to stay on track.

Write one goal for each of the areas listed below. If you have never thought about your goals before, don't rush through this. Give plenty of thought to your hopes, dreams, and values. What is really important to you? What do you want?

Education Goal:_____

_____ Target date: _____

Job/Career Goal:_____

_____ Target date: _____

Health/Fitness Goal:_____

_____ Target date: _____

Social/Friendship Goal:_____

_____ Target date: _____

Family Goal:_____

_____ Target date: _____

Personal Goal:_____

_____ Target date: _____

Control Time-Wasters

It has been said that, "You waste your time whenever you spend it doing something *less* important when you could be doing something *more* important." Do you agree with that statement? Why or why not?

To find out whether or not an activity is a time-waster for you, measure it against your goals. Is the activity helping you reach your goals? If not, how can you reduce or eliminate the time you devote to it?

Put a check (✔) beside your time-wasters.

___ **Cluttered work area**. Get as much clutter off your work or study surface as you possibly can. Throw worthless scraps into the trash basket. Quickly move along items that have to go to someone else. Don't let paper and "stuff" pile up. Spending a few minutes each week (or at the end of each day) cleaning up clutter can make you more productive. Use some sort of filing system to keep the important things organized.

___ **Lack of necessary materials or equipment**. How much time do you waste looking for things you need, but either don't have or can't find? If you share equipment with others, agree to return items to a central location when not in use.

___ **Interruptions**. Two main sources of interruptions are the phone and visitors. Try to limit your receipt of calls to certain periods of time. Return messages during a planned block of time. Keep phone conversations short. When possible, send a short email or text message instead of phoning. To control visitors, use some sort of signal to let people know that you don't want to be interrupted. Hang a sign on the entrance to your work or study area. That lets others know you're working or studying and that you don't want to be interrupted.

___ **Socializing**. At work it's important to be friendly with your coworkers, and you may even make friends with some of the people with whom you work. But you're getting paid to work, not socialize. Plan to get together with the people you enjoy after work or on weekends.

___ **Uncertainty — not knowing what to do**. Good planning helps you know exactly what to do and when to do it. Planning also helps you decide what to do next when you've finished one task and no one is around to direct you to a new one. Use a daily planner to keep yourself on track with responsibilities, specific assignments, and daily or weekly plans. Refer often to your goals.

___ **Daydreaming**. First figure out why you daydream. Is it because you don't have enough to do? If so, concentrate on improving your planning. Is it because you're bored? Then take responsibility for finding ways to make things more interesting for yourself. Challenge yourself to do things *better*, or *faster*, or simply do *more*. If your daydreaming is caused by lack of discipline, you have two choices: Either become your own watchdog (which in itself takes discipline) or ask someone for help. A friend or family member could signal you when you appear to be off in the ozone.

___ **Procrastination**. Most of us tend to put off things that are unpleasant, things that are difficult, and things that involve tough decisions. These are often the very things that contribute most to our success! Try these procrastination fighters:

• Do unpleasant tasks first. Or do them in small pieces, setting a deadline for each.

• Break down difficult tasks into smaller parts. Keep breaking down the parts until you see the doable pieces.

• Get more information. A task may seem difficult simply because you don't know enough about it. The more you know, the more likely you are to become interested and involved.

How Do You Manage Your Time?

How often do you sit down and plan your school or work activities in writing?

___ daily   ___ weekly   ___ monthly   ___ not at all

What specific steps can you take to improve in the area of planning?

_____

_____

Do you prioritize your activities, and complete your most important activities first?

      Always   Sometimes   Never

What can you do to improve in the area of prioritizing?

_____

What is your biggest time waster? _____

What can you do to reduce or eliminate this time waster? _____

_____

Do you seem to have enough time to complete your work? If not, why not?

_____

_____

Do you feel productive and in control? If not, what ideas can you come up with that will enable you to gain control of your life and commitments?

_____

_____

_____

_____

_____

Respecting Expertise, Experience and Authority

Expertise is another name for the knowledge and skill possessed by an expert, or by a person who knows a lot about a particular subject. People develop expertise through:
- formal education
- training programs
- independent reading and study
- practice

Experience is gained by doing something repeatedly. The more years a person is actively involved in a particular job or profession, the more experience the person accumulates. Experience (practice) by itself can build expertise, even without formal education or training, but this is not always the case.

Authority is the power to make decisions and to direct the activities of others. The person with authority in a particular situation is the person in charge. For example, a teacher has authority in the classroom, while the principal has authority over the entire school. Parents have authority at home, but a hired baby-sitter has authority while they are away. At a particular company, a supervisor has authority over a group of workers, a division manager over several supervisors, and the company president over everyone who works for the company.

Respect Has Its Reasons

Why does it make sense to respect the opinion of a person who has expertise in a particular field?

_____

_____

_____

Why do people with many years of experience deserve respect?

_____

_____

Think of a person you respect who has authority over you. Why do you respect that person?

_____

_____

How do you show your respect?

_____

_____

What could you learn from a person who has had many years of experience:

• teaching children? _____

• supporting a family? _____

• running a business? _____

• cooking? _____

• installing electrical systems? _____

• working for one boss? _____

• volunteering in a hospital? _____

Deciding Who Can Help You

- Assuming you had the money to pay, whom would you be most likely to hire to build a set of storage cabinets in your garage:
    - —a licensed carpenter with 7 years of experience
    - —your neighbor who built a similar cabinet in her own garage last year
    - —a handyman whose ad lists 25 years experience in household building and repairs

- Assuming you could pay, whom would you hire to repair your computer:
    - —a service company licensed by the manufacturer to repair your brand of computer
    - —a student who is currently studying computer maintenance and repair
    - —a member of your computer-users group who has been helping other members with programming and repair problems for 15 years

- Imagine you are a newly hired salesperson at a large department store. Who do you think could **best** assist you if:
    - —you wanted to know how to fill out your time card
    - —you wanted to talk to someone who had a lot of practice dealing with dissatisfied customers
    - —a customer asked you to find out if Case Cosmetics had a specific color of lipstick in stock
    - —you wanted to learn more about the income levels and fashion preferences of customers
    - —a customer wanted to pay with a gift certificate and you didn't know the procedure

    1. the salesperson with the most years of experience
    2. the representative from the Case Cosmetics Company
    3. the supervisor of your department
    4. the other clerk at your register
    5. the marketing specialist in the business office upstairs

- You are a paid intern at a full-service pet hospital and kennel, practicing to be a veterinarian's assistant. Who do you think could **best** assist you if:
    - —you needed to change your work schedule during final exam week at school
    - —a pet owner asked which shampoo wouldn't irritate her dog's skin problem
    - —you observed a cat in recovery from surgery begin to tremble violently
    - —you wanted to know more about the responsibilities a vet's assistant handles on a long-term basis
    - —customers kept asking questions about the hospital's vaccination program that you couldn't answer

    1. the pet groomer and trainer
    2. the veterinarian
    3. the office manager
    4. a vet's assistant with 3 years of experience

Working with Different Styles of Authority

A person in authority has the right and the responsibility to make decisions and to see that those decisions are carried out. That includes giving directions to other people — telling them what to do. Different people express their authority in different ways. They have different "styles."

It's important to learn to work with different authority styles, because every boss you will ever have will be different. However, respect is something that a person in authority must always be shown, regardless of his or her style.

Here are examples of those different authority styles. Read through each description and think carefully about what it would be like to work for each one.

Dominant Dan: Dan tells people what to do and then he watches closely to make sure they do it. He sets clear rules and procedures; those who follow them get rewards and those who don't get called on the carpet. When you work for Dan, you always know who is in charge.

What would be good about working for Dan?

_____

_____

_____

_____

_____

_____

What would be challenging about working for Dan?

_____

_____

_____

_____

_____

_____

Cooperative Chris: Chris likes to involve others and give them opportunities to express their opinions and share their ideas. When a decision has to be made, Chris often asks others what they think. She listens and considers their opinions before making her decision. Sometimes she allows them to make the decision. Chris would rather make suggestions and requests than give orders. Although Chris is clearly in charge, people who work for her know that she expects them to show initiative and stay involved.

What would be good about working for Chris?

_____

_____

_____

_____

_____

_____

What would be challenging about working for Chris?

_____

_____

_____

_____

_____

Uninvolved Irv: Irv assumes everyone knows his or her job and is doing it. He is usually too busy with his own work to pay much attention to anyone else's. When a problem occurs, Irv assumes his people will find a solution. If someone asks him for direction, he usually says something like, "Do whatever you think is best." When a decision needs to be made, he often delegates. In other words, he asks one or more of his people to choose a course of action. He almost always accepts their decision.

What would be good about working for Irv

_____

_____

_____

_____

_____

_____

What would be challenging about working for Irv?

_____

_____

_____

_____

_____

Interview A Working Person

Identify someone you know who is or has been in the workforce. Learn as much as you can by interviewing this person about his or her experience and how he or she relates to those in authority. Ask these questions:

Position of person being interviewed: _____

How many years of experience have you had in this field?_____

How long have you been working for this organization? _____

How long have you held your current position? _____

How did you achieve your current position? _____

_____

Who has authority over you? _____

_____

How do you show respect for the person(s) who has authority over you?

_____

_____

Which people in the organization do you go to for advice and assistance, and what are their areas of expertise?

_____

_____

Which people have been working for this organization the longest, and how does their experience help you?

_____

_____

What did *you* learn from this interview?

_____

_____

Proving
Your
Dependability

Target:

The activities in this section will help you:

▷ examine personal experiences dealing with dependable and undependable individuals.

▷ make a habit of exceeding people's expectations.

▷ look for opportunities to develop additional skills, and to "gets things done."

People Are Watching!

Being dependable means showing others that they can depend on you to fulfill your obligations, work cooperatively with others, and contribute to achieving goals. Dependability implies being responsible — actively *responding* to people and situations that need attention. It implies keeping commitments, and not letting others down.

In many companies, the first several weeks of employment are considered probationary. Probation is a period of time during which a person's fitness for employment is tested. Proving to others that you are a responsible, dependable employee doesn't happen overnight. It requires consistent positive action for as long as the probationary period lasts.

One of the fastest, most effective ways to prove your dependability is to always do a little more than is expected of you. If Friday is the deadline for your report, submit it on Thursday. If you are expected to close ten sales, make twelve your goal. If getting an order packaged and out the door usually takes three days, do it in two and a half. Give a little more, a little faster, a little better.

Let Your Own Experience Guide You

Think of someone you depend on. How does that person show you that he or she is dependable?

_____

_____

_____

_____

Have you ever known a person who was unreliable? What made you decide that you couldn't rely on that person?

_____

_____

_____

_____

How do you feel when someone you depend on lets you down?

_____

_____

_____

_____

Think of a time when someone failed to keep an agreement with you. How did you feel about that person?

_____

_____

_____

_____

What An Employer Appreciates

Put yourself in an employer's position. Would you feel you could depend on

a person who: or a person who:

— missed a lot of work. . . . . .was always there

— often arrived late . . . . arrived on time or a few
                                                           minutes early

— failed to complete assignments . . . . .turned in finished work on
                                                           time

— frequently misunderstood instructions . . . . .listened and followed
                                                           instructions correctly

— seemed to get confused . . . . .always seemed to grasp
                                                           what was going on

— acted uninterested in his or her work . . . . . . showed enthusiasm for his
                                                           or her work

— talked behind your back . . . . demonstrated respect for
                                                           you

— complained all the time . . . . .had a positive attitude

— gossiped about coworkers . . . . .appreciated and respected
                                                           coworkers

— blamed someone or something else
   every time things went wrong . . . . admitted his or her mistakes
                                                           and learned from them

— always had an excuse . . . . accepted responsibility

What other ways can you think of to have an employer appreciate and have
confidence in you?

_____

_____

_____

_____

How to "Stand Out" on the Job

Be Someone Who Can "Take Care of It"

The more different tasks you can "take care of" in a job, the more valuable you become. Look for opportunities to develop related skills that can be used in situations other than the ones that come up in your regular job.

For example, if your current job is to do billing, see what you can learn about other office procedures, such as ordering and scheduling. If you drive a delivery truck, learn how the warehouse is organized. If you work in retail sales, find out about inventory control and the responsibilities of your company's buyers.

Be a team member who can play different positions in the game. Then, when someone is needed to fill in, let your supervisor know that you can "take care of it."

Do What's Expected, and Then Some

Do more than your job description requires. Volunteer to help out whenever you can. If your employer asks you to work on holidays, do so if at all possible. If a coworker needs to trade shifts, offer to help out. Call regular customers to let them know when items they might like are going on sale.

Look for the little things that go undone because they're not part of *anyone's* job description. For example:

- If you see miscellaneous product manuals lying around everywhere, organize them into a set of three-ring binders.

- Straighten up a supply shelf that's in disarray.

- If a procedure isn't working as well as it might, tactfully suggest a way to improve it.

- Tidy up the foyer or waiting room when you notice that it's messy.

- Bring in something to share with your coworkers, like a snack, flowers, house plant, inspirational quotation, or cartoon.

Working Cooperatively with Others

Target:

The activities in this section will help you:

⇨ assess your ability to get along with others.

⇨ prepare to be a valued member of work teams.

⇨ understand the problems that groups face as they work together.

⇨ cope with difficult people.

⇨ practice helpful verbal responses to use when working with others.

What Are Interpersonal Skills?

Specific job-skill requirements vary from job to job, but the need to get along with other people is universal. Good interpersonal skills include the willingness and ability to accept and respect others, communicate, cooperate, share, and work together to complete projects, solve problems, and resolve conflicts.

It's not always easy to work with other people. Some individuals have annoying habits that get on your nerves. They talk too much, joke around all the time, or seem moody or argumentative. Still, it's up to *you* to make the best of your work situation.

Occasionally — or perhaps regularly — you'll be expected to collaborate with a team of other employees on a specific task or project. Developing real teamwork takes time and effort, but the payoffs can be huge. More ideas, greater creativity, better decisions, increased commitment, higher productivity, and stronger relationships are a few of the payoffs.

How Well Do You Get Along with Others?

• Recall a time you worked on a school project with two or more other students. How did you divide up the work? _____

What happened when you disagreed with each other? _____

_____

How satisfied were you with the finished project? _____

What did you learn about working with others from this experience?

_____

_____

• Rate yourself as a group member. Think about a specific group you've been a member of (club, athletic team, etc.) as you consider and check (✔) each item.

	always	sometimes	never
I listen actively to others.			
I respect and consider other people's ideas.			
I stick with the decisions of the group.			
I do my share of the work.			
I accept and learn from criticism.			
I offer to help others when they run into problems.			
I let others know I appreciate their work.			
I willingly share credit with other group members.			

• Describe two specific ways you can improve your ability to work with others.

1. Desired improvement: _____

Steps I can take: _____

_____

_____

2. Desired improvement: _____

Steps I can take: _____

_____

_____

Becoming A Team

Six students (or employees) who sit at different desks, work on individual assignments, and receive separate evaluations are not a team. However, when those students or employees sit around a table and work on a project together, they start to become a team.

If you've ever been on a softball team, football team, soccer team, debate team, cheer leading team, or any other kind of team, you know that "teamwork" doesn't just happen. It takes time, effort, and practice for a group of people to function like a true team.

A highly effective team —like a champion volleyball or basketball team — works together smoothly and cooperatively. Every person is respected, the skills and talents of each member are utilized, problems are solved jointly, and everyone works toward the same goal. When a group functions like this, it's a team.

Stages of Group Development

As a group works together, it goes through certain stages of development — much like a child goes through different stages as he or she grows up.

Stage 1: The team looks for leadership and directions.

Members look at each other and ask, "What are we supposed to do?" They feel somewhat confused. Maybe they ask their teacher or boss for help. At some point, however, they realize that if they're going to be a team, they have to start acting like one.

Stage 2: The team starts to organize. Conflicts emerge and are settled.

How do members act like a team? Well first, they have to figure out all the different parts of the job. They have to answer the "who," "what," "when," "where," and "how" questions that are part of getting organized. In the process, members sometimes disagree about who should do things and how they should be done.

Stage 3: Information flows freely and members feel good about the team.

By the time it reaches this stage, the team is organized and conflicts have been settled. Members find themselves working together extremely well. They still disagree sometimes, but now conflicts are seen as natural and members have found effective ways to resolve them.

Stage 4: The team can solve problems. Members are interdependent.

At this stage, the team seems capable of tackling anything. Creative ideas flow easily. Members work alone, in pairs, or as a total group with equal success. Every member of the team is valued and is depended upon by every other member.

Think again about a group or team to which you have belonged. Look back at the "Stages of Group Development." In your opinion, which stage did this group reach? What specific incidents and/or group behaviors support your conclusion?

Coping with Difficult People on the Job

When you're in the workplace, you'll encounter many people. They will each have their own personalities and ways of relating to others. Some people will be more difficult than others to get along with Here are some typical annoying behaviors and what you can do to effectively cope with them:

The Know-It-All. Don't waste your time arguing with a "know-it-all." Instead, listen with interest and patience. Ask lots of questions about the person's ideas or ways of doing things. Try to slip your own ideas in through your questions and comments. For example:

"Have you ever tried solving that problem by...?"

"That's a good idea. We could try that, and maybe as a variation we could..."

"What do you think would happen if we...?"

The Tease. If someone teases you, ignore it or tease back, and try not to be too bothered by the teasing. If you *are* bothered, try not to show it. Some people will tease you even more if they know that it bothers you. If none of these methods works, tell your supervisor about the problem. This is not the same as tattling; you're telling your supervisor something that he or she should know. Besides, it's best to discuss problems before they get worse.

The Nosy Questioner. Don't be surprised to find yourself working with at least one person who asks all kinds of unwelcome questions. You don't have to answer questions about your personal life. Here are some possible responses:

"Why do you ask?"

"I'd rather not say."

"I prefer not to answer personal questions."

The Gossip. Rumors make their rounds in most organizations, and usually they're harmless. Unfortunately though, most organizations also have their "professional rumormongers" — individuals who seem to delight in whispering behind people's backs, spreading gossip, and creating tension and turmoil. Whether they do it for power, attention, revenge, or out of jealousy, you may have to deal with their actions.

Don't repeat rumors or be drawn into gossip. Better yet, do your part to stop rumors. One way is to say, "I've heard that too, but it's only a rumor." If you are the victim of gossip, try to ignore it — rumors tend to die quickly. If the rumor is vicious or interferes with your ability to do your job, talk to your supervisor.

Sexual Harassment. Biased people are everywhere. Ignore them. Don't laugh at their jokes or respond to their suggestive comments. Don't participate in a conversation that's not related to business.

Comments, invitations, and touching become harassment *the very first time* they make you feel uncomfortable or interfere with your ability to do your job. If a person comes on to you by using familiar language ("sweetheart, cutie, honey") tell the person that you don't like those terms and want to be addressed by your name. Be assertive the *first time* it happens. If a person hints at "getting together," change the subject immediately to something business-related. If the hint becomes an invitation, firmly and clearly state that you're not interested. Don't waste time explaining yourself. No is no. If the behavior continues, tell your supervisor immediately.

How Do YOU Handle Difficult People

Think about the people with whom you interact. In your mind, identify the person who is the *hardest* to be with.

What does that person do that makes being with him or her difficult?

_____

_____

How do you normally react to this person? What do you say and do?

_____

_____

If you had outstanding interpersonal skills and were in complete control of the situation, how would you react?

_____

_____

Describe two specific things can you begin doing immediately to improve your way of reacting to this person.

1. _____

_____

_____

_____

2. _____

_____

_____

_____

_____

Practice Your Lines

Why should actors be the only ones with scripts? If you want to deliver a great performance in your job while getting along well with others, learn effective things to say and when to say them. Here are a few possibilities.

Expressing your desire to cooperate:

Is there any way I can help out?
What can I do for you today?
I want us to work on this together.
We all have the same goal.
I support you on that idea.
Let's all try to think of solutions.

Complimenting and meeting coworkers:

You did a great job!
Good thinking!
I can learn a lot by watching you.
Excuse me. I've seen you several times and I'd like to introduce myself. I'm . . ., and I work over in...
I noticed you at the meeting the other day. My name is . . .. May I ask your name?
You seem to know a lot about this business. I hope we get a chance to work together on a project some time.

Showing interest and concern:

What is your opinion on this?
I understand the situation.
How's your work going?
I'd like to learn more about what you do.
Sounds like you had a rough morning
If there's anything I can do, please let me know.

Coping when things go wrong

I'm sorry. What should I do now?
How can we fix this matter?
I'll work on it until I get it right.
I can see you're upset. Can we talk?
There must be a solution to this problem.
Arguing about this won't help. Let's work together to find the best answer.

Asking for help or clarification:

Would you please check this to make sure I'm on the right track?
Did I understand you to say . . .?
Is this the right way to do it?
I didn't understand the last part of your instructions. Would you mind repeating them?
Here are two ideas. Which one do you think is best?
This problem has me stumped. Can you help?

A Worker's Creed

- I don't make fun of other people.

- I do not judge people by their race, ethnic group, or religion.

- I don't spread gossip.

- I mind my own business.

- I don't get into arguments or fights.

- I try to be friendly to everyone.

- I show respect for my employer and coworkers.

- I work cooperatively and hard.

Valuing the Contributions of Coworkers

Tales of Two Workplaces

Rachel worked at a large and very busy quick-copy store. There were usually at least six employees like Rachel working in the store at any one time, servicing customers, filling out order forms, and using the big copy machines to complete large orders. Rachel knew how important it was to listen carefully to each customer's instructions. She'd been there when angry customers returned to the store complaining that their printing was done incorrectly. In the first six months that Rachel worked for the store, she never made a mistake; however, no one ever seemed to notice her good work. Then one day she printed a very large order on the wrong paper. The unhappy customer chewed out Rachel's coworker who had taken the order and then talked to the store manager. Finally, both the manager and the coworker reprimanded Rachel harshly and were cold toward her for the remainder of the day. Rachel felt badly about her mistake, but angry that her boss and coworker had made such a big deal of it. She resented having received so much attention for her mistake, and almost none for her hard work. Rachel's enthusiasm for her job went into a long, slow slide. She grew less careful and made more mistakes. After about three months, Rachel quit her job.

Do you think Rachel's good work during the first six months was appreciated by her coworkers? ...by the store manager?

_____

_____

_____

_____

_____

Why did Rachel lose her commitment and eventually quit her job?

_____

_____

_____

_____

_____

Recall a time when you achieved a goal, accomplished a task, or did something considerate for someone, and no one seemed to notice. How did you feel?

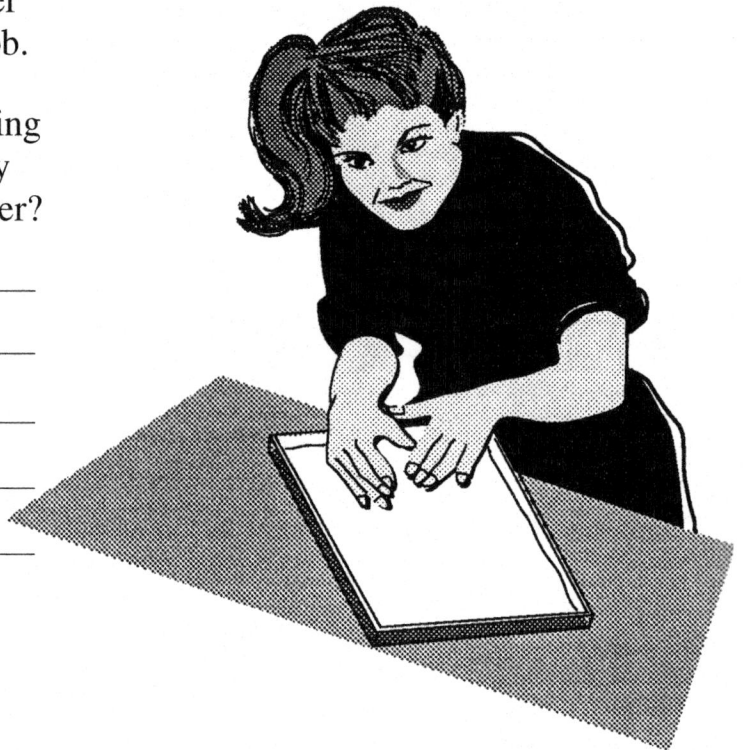

_____

_____

_____

_____

_____

_____

C raig was hired as a trainee in a large landscaping company. Most of the company's customers were big apartment and condominium complexes and office buildings. Craig was learning to design and install automated sprinkling systems, and was currently in charge of checking and repairing several existing ones. Craig loved being outdoors most of the time. The employees worked in teams with a supervisor. Craig's supervisor expected her crew to work hard and fast, but she placed greater emphasis on getting excellent results. She never failed to praise a crew member for doing a good job, whether it was designing, planting, trimming, weeding, mowing, or, in Craig's case, watering. The crew took such pride in its performance that members noticed each other's work, too, and the compliments flowed in all directions.

One day Craig's supervisor had to leave her crew and make an emergency run to another site. When she caught up with the crew at the end of the day, she called Craig aside. She told him that a serious error had been made in the programming of a sprinkler system at a large condominium complex. By the time the residents had discovered the problem, their water bill had gone sky high and an enormous amount of water had been wasted. When Craig realized his error, he felt awful. His supervisor was stern as she said, "Craig, I've been very pleased with your progress and I really enjoy working with you, but this kind of mistake can't be allowed to happen again. What can we do to make sure it doesn't?" Later she got the whole crew together to talk about the problem and come up with a system for double checking Craig's programming. Everyone focused on solving the problem and no one tried to make Craig feel any worse than he already did. Craig stayed with the company and became one of its top landscape architects, and he never forgot what he learned from his first supervisor.

How did Craig's supervisor get her crew to take pride in their work?

_____

_____

_____

_____

What was most effective about the way the supervisor handled Craig's mistake?

_____

_____

_____

_____

Think of a time when someone expressed appreciation for you or something you did. How did you feel?

_____

_____

_____

_____

_____

_____

_____

_____

Praise Is Like a Virus — Powerful and Contagious

In the field of psychology, it's called *positive reinforcement*. When a task is done right, the behavior is rewarded immediately. The reward reinforces the correct behavior, making it more likely that behavior will be repeated. Praise, compliments, and appreciation are among the most powerful forms of positive reinforcement.

When you notice and appreciate each person's talents, abilities, and contributions, you accomplish several things:
- You cause people to feel good.
- You positively reinforce (encourage more) of the same behavior.
- You help create a positive atmosphere in your workplace, in school, on teams, or anyplace else you are together with others.
- By modeling appreciative behavior, you teach others how to show their appreciation for you and each other.

What You Give, You Get Back — Always!

You may have heard this belief expressed a little differently, with the phrase, "What goes around comes around." Very simply, it means that however you treat others is how *you* will be treated in the long run. So if you want to be valued and appreciated, value and appreciate everyone else around you. It works!

Do It in Writing

When you want to make your expressions of appreciation even more powerful, put them in writing. When a coworker does something especially thoughtful, put a handwritten note on his or her desk. Or send an email to a coworker. When a customer makes a special purchase, send a note of congratulations and thanks. Always send a thank-you letter immediately after a job interview.

Be Sincere

In order to effectively show appreciation, you first have to *feel* it. Phony praise seldom fools anyone. Pay attention. Make a habit of *noticing* and *valuing* the contributions that other people make. When you feel it first, your praise will always ring true.

How to Express Your Appreciation

One of the most effective ways to express your positive feelings and thoughts is with an I-statement. An I-statement allows you to "own" whatever you are saying. It's *your* observation. It's *your* opinion. I-statements also tend to give the listener more information than do statements of praise. Look at these examples:

I-statement:	**Praise:**
I really like the way you formatted that report. It was easy to read and pleasing to look at.	*Great report!*
I enjoy working with you because you always pitch in and do your part.	*You're a terrific partner.*

To make an I-statement, just follow these steps:
1. Begin with the word "I."
2. State how you feel or what you think.
3. Describe what the person did to earn your positive thoughts and feelings.

Who did something today that helped you in school or in your job?

_____

What did he or she do? _____

_____

_____

Did you express your appreciation? Why/Why not?

_____

_____

If not, what could you have said to the person? Write an I-statement here:

_____

_____

_____

_____

Take a Contributions Inventory

In the space below, list the names of people with whom you closely interact. Next to each name, list at least one talent, skill, trait, or characteristic that you appreciate in that person. If you can't *sincerely* think of anything to write, wait. Spend the next few days paying careful attention to that person. Then, after you've discovered something you *truly* appreciate, complete your list.

Name	What I Appreciate
_____	_____
	_____
_____	_____
	_____
_____	_____
	_____
_____	_____
	_____
_____	_____
	_____
_____	_____
	_____
_____	_____
	_____

Giving Great Customer Service

Target:

The activities in this section will help you learn:

▷ who your customers are.

▷ how customers react to different kinds of responses.

▷ the do's and don'ts of satisfying customer needs.

▷ how to work with difficult customers.

▷ how to make up for mistakes.

What Do Customers Want?

Most customers are not very hard to please. They expect to be treated with respect and to get results. Always try to give them:

• Reliability

Be there to help customers when they need it. Give accurate information. If you promise to check on something and get back to a customer, do it — as promptly as possible.

• Responsiveness

Try not to keep customers waiting. Listen carefully to what they say (or ask) and respond thoughtfully. If you don't have an answer, get one from your supervisor as quickly as possible.

• Assurance

Don't be wishy-washy. Express confidence in your own and the company's ability to give customers the product or service they desire.

• Understanding

Listen and try to understand the customer's point of view. Show empathy.

Customer Watch

Spend at least twenty minutes in a local place of business. Choose a business where customers are receiving service, such as a restaurant, dry cleaners, movie theater, department store or supermarket checkout. Listen to the comments made by customers to at least **two different employees** (more if you like). Take notes. Notice and record how each employee responds.

Employee A

Company:

Position:

Customer Comment	Employee Reaction

Employee B

Company:

Position:

Customer Comment	Employee Reaction

Making Customers Feel Like Number One

The do's

✔ Listen. Give customers your undivided attention.

✔ Be friendly, without being intimate. Keep a respectful distance.

✔ Be on the alert for signs that a customer isn't completely satisfied.

You look a little puzzled. Is there something I can help you with?

You don't seem sure about this. Would you like to speak to ...?

✔ Say things that let your customers know that their satisfaction is your top priority.

Please don't hesitate to ask me questions.

Is there anything else at all that I can get you?

✔ Try not to upset a customer when delivering bad news.

I'm really sorry, but that shipment hasn't come in. We're expecting it before closing today. May I call you immediately or have the item shipped to your home?

The don'ts

Actions often speak louder and more clearly than words. You can turn a customer off very quickly with a sigh or a shrug, or just by the expression on your face. Be very careful never to do anything that conveys one of these messages:

1. I don't know.

2. I don't care.

3. Don't bother me; I'm too busy for you.

4. I don't like you.

5. I know more than you do.

6. You don't know what you're talking about.

7. Your kind isn't welcome here (prejudice).

8. We don't need you.

Describe a difficult situation involving a customer.

If you do not work directly with the public, interview a friend who does.

Describe the situation.

_____

_____

_____

_____

_____

_____

How did you/your friend handle the situation?

_____

_____

_____

_____

_____

_____

What was the result of this action?

_____

_____

_____

_____

_____

What will you/your friend do differently the next time you experience this type of situation?

_____

_____

_____

_____

Why?

_____

_____

_____

_____

Handling Difficult Customers:

Here are some typical customer "types". Think about constructive ways of handling customers like these. Write down your ideas.

1. She is angry, and blames her problems on you. She says things to make you feel small. When you try to stand up for yourself, she threatens to report you to your boss.

   _____

   _____

   _____

2. He wants to visit with you. He forces you to keep other customers waiting while he chats. When you try to close the conversation, he starts to get annoyed.

   _____

   _____

   _____

3. She demands red-carpet service. She wants you to drop everything for her — meetings, other customers, your lunch break. She expects extras, like discounts, free delivery, the best seat or table, and lots of personal attention.

   _____

   _____

   _____

4. He knows more than you do about everything, especially the product or service you are selling. He argues with every statement you make. You're sure that he's trying to make you look stupid.

   _____

   _____

OOOPS!

Everybody makes mistakes. Think of a time when you goofed, and someone got upset. Describe your error:

_____

_____

_____

What did the other person do?

_____

_____

How did you respond? _____

_____

_____

_____

What happened in the end? _____

_____

_____

How to Regain a Customer's Trust

When you make a mistake on the job:

1. Apologize.

2. Listen to the person's feelings and let him or her know that you understand.

3. Fix the problem quickly.

4. If possible, do something extra to make up for the customer's inconvenience.

5. Keep your word. Do everything you say you will do.

6. Follow up to make sure that the customer is completely satisfied.

Be Prepared!

When you have a job, ask your supervisor what kinds of things the company does to make amends for its mistakes. Depending on the type of business, little extras might include:
—a free dessert
—a lower price
—free delivery
—a discount coupon or free pass
—a gift certificate

_____

_____

_____

_____

_____

Making Effective Decisions

You Are Always Deciding

Do you have trouble discriminating between big decisions and little decisions? Does practically every decision seem like a big one? If so, you may not realize just how many decisions you actually make.

You make decisions every day. Many are quick, easy decisions like what to eat and what to wear. Others are more involved, like deciding what subject to write a report on. Still others are very important, like deciding whether or not to pursue a particular career.

Generally speaking, the more important the decision, the more conscious effort you need to devote to making it. Good decision making involves using information to make choices. Information about:
—your values and goals
—people and things that influence you
—the various alternatives you have
—the likely consequences of choosing each alternative

Target:

The activities in this section will help you:

➪ learn and practice a step-by-step decision-making process.

➪ distinguish between decisions and outcomes.

➪ assess the effects on decision making of stress and ability to handle risks.

➪ examine recent decisions and their outcomes.

Using What You Know to Get What You Want

The decision-making process involves using what you know (or can learn) to get what you want. Here are some steps to follow when you have a decision to make:

1. Recognize and define the decision to be made.
2. Know what is important to you — your goals and values.
3. Study the information you have already; obtain and study new information, too.
4. List all of your alternatives.
5. List the advantages and disadvantages of each alternative.
6. Make a decision.
7. Develop a plan for carrying out your decision.

Problems with Decisions

✔ If you have trouble coming up with alternatives, it could be because you don't have enough information. Try making a list of questions about the decision. Then, spend some time getting answers to those questions. In the process, you'll increase your alternatives.

✔ If you feel you have *too* many alternatives to choose from, limit them. One way to do this is to test each alternative against your goals and values. Then eliminate the ones that either don't help you reach your goals or aren't in keeping with your values (what's important to you).

✔ If you can't tell which alternatives are better than others, talk to someone about them.

Decision or Outcome?

Next time you're tempted to kick yourself over a "bad" decision, consider this:

- When you say that a decision is poor, you probably mean the *result* or *outcome* is not what you wanted.
- Good decision making minimizes the possibility of getting bad outcomes, but it doesn't eliminate the possibility.
- A *decision* is the act of choosing among several possibilities based on your judgments.
- An *outcome* is the result, consequence, or aftermath of the decision.
- You have direct control over the decision, but not over the outcome.
- A good decision does not guarantee a good outcome, but it does increase the chances of a good outcome.

What is the worst decision you ever made? Was it really a bad decision, or was it a reasonable decision with a bad outcome?

Testing the Process

Find out how the decision-making process really works. Think of a decision that you need to make during the next month. Then answer these questions:

1. What outcome do you want from this decision? _____
_____

2. What kinds of things that are important in your life (your goals and values) might affect, or be affected by, this decision?
_____

3. What kinds of information do you have and/or need to make the best decisions?

Things to think about: _____

_____

Things to read: _____

_____

People to talk to: _____

_____

Things to do: _____

_____

4. List your alternatives and the advantages and disadvantages of each.

Alternative	Advantages	Disadvantages

Decision Point!
Which alternative has the best chance of producing the outcome you want?

Why Decisions Are Sometimes Stressful

Ever get upset and anxious when faced with a decision? You're not alone. Lots of people do. One way to meet the stress head-on is to figure out what's causing it. Study this list of possible causes, and thinking back to an important decision that was stressful for you, check (✔) the ones that applied to you.

____ I'm afraid I'll make the wrong decision.
____ I don't understand the choices.
____ If I choose one thing, I'll have to give up something else.
____ I don't like any of the alternatives.
____ I'm worried about pleasing someone else.
____ I'm not very confident of my ability to decide.
____ Since I don't know what I want, it's hard to make a decision.
____ I usually choose the first alternative that comes up.

When Making Tough Decisions, Look at the Risks

Since you can never completely control the outcome of a decision, there's always a risk that the alternative you choose may fail.

In selecting from among alternatives, it helps to determine how much of a risk you are willing to take. Some people are big risk-takers. They choose the alternative that offers the most desirable outcome no matter how risky it is. For example, Sam applies for the highest paying job, even though there's more competition and he just barely qualifies. Other people always play it safe. They choose the alternative that involves the lowest risk, even though the outcome may be mediocre. Dave applies for a job that doesn't look very interesting or pay very much, but will be pretty easy to land. Between these two extremes is the person who is willing to take some risks, but weighs the odds carefully. Juanita applies for a job that pays a reasonably good salary, and for which she is qualified. She decides that she has about a 60% chance of being hired.

When choosing from among alternatives, always eliminate any option that might present a loss you won't be able to live with.

Think back over the recent important decisions you've made. How high a risk have you usually been willing to take?

No Risk	1	2	3	4	5	6	7	8	9	10	Extremely High Risk

Making A Good Decision

Describe a decision that you've recently had to make.

_____

_____

_____

Describe how you went about making the decision.

_____

_____

_____

How difficult was it to make the decision?
___ difficult ___ easy ___ routine

How important was the decision?
___ very important ___ somewhat important ___ not very important

How did your decision turn out?
___ It turned out very well. I made the best possible decision.
___ I made what I thought was a good decision, but it didn't turn out as well
    as I expected.

The next time you have a decision to make, what will you do that can help
in your decision-making process?

_____

_____

_____

_____

_____

_____

_____

_____

The Decision Agent

When it's especially important to make a good decision, people often ask someone to help them. They might use a stockbroker, a lawyer, a doctor, or an architect for certain difficult decisions. **Imagine a new kind of expert.** Instead of a stockbroker who is an expert on investments, or an architect who is an expert on designing, assume that there is a **"decision agent"**—an expert on decision making. You can employ a decision agent to make your decisions for you.

To learn something about yourself and about the decisions that are important to you, answer these questions, and think about your reasoning behind your answers.

Pretend your city has a limited number of "decision agents". You can assign only three decisions in your life to the agent. *Which three would you assign?*

1. _____
2. _____
3. _____

Assume that your city requires you to assign *all* of the decisions in your life *except* three to a decision agent. *Which three would you not assign?*

1. _____
2. _____
3. _____

For each decision in the first question, what instruction would you give your decision agent? Why?

1. _____

_____

2. _____

_____

3. _____

_____

Taking Assignments All the Way

Target:

The activities in this section will help you:

➡ approach assignments with a workable plan.

➡ apply discipline and avoid "perfection paralysis."

➡ develop "matrix thinking" to clarify objectives and tasks.

➡ consider personal motivations.

On Time and in Top Form

Some people rarely complete an assignment on time. If you give them a week, they take two. If you give them six months, they take nine.

Other people get their projects finished on time, but their work is sloppy. Ironically, looking at their work, you'd almost be willing to wager they didn't have enough time! In fact, they didn't *take* enough time.

An assignment is a commitment. Even if you don't actually *choose* the assignment — even if it's forced on you — it's still a commitment. And the commitment is twofold. First, you've promised to do it (that means *all* of it); second you've promised to get it done (that means *finish* it).

Don't rush into an assignment. Take the time you need to study similar projects and discuss your findings and ideas with your coworkers and supervisor. Or, if it's a school assignment, talk with your teacher and other students. Then plan. Be sure you:

✔ understand the assignment
✔ have the tools for the assignment
✔ have a picture of the time requirements
✔ schedule the work
✔ motivate yourself
✔ discipline yourself

How Disciplined Are You Now?

Completing assignments doesn't have as much to do with intelligence (you have enough) or knowledge (you can get the information you need) as it does with creating a schedule and sticking to it. If you do fall behind, and it looks as though you can't meet your deadline, inform your supervisor or teacher *ahead of time*. Revise the schedule, make a new commitment, and go for it.

How good are you at completing school assignments? _____

_____

Do you get your school assignments completed on time? If not, what are your favorite excuses?

_____

_____

Do you ever rush through assignments, finishing them on time but shortchanging the quality? If so, what do you need to learn?

____ to take greater pride in my work
____ to think more about the assignment and less about what I'm going to do afterwards
____ to reread and rewrite
____ to ask another person to check over my work and make suggestions
____ to make a detailed plan before I start

When was the last time you suffered from "perfection paralysis?" (You couldn't seem to get started on an assignment because you were afraid you wouldn't do a perfect job.) Did you ever finish the assignment? If so, how did it turn out?

_____

_____

_____

_____

Protect Yourself from "Perfection Paralysis"

One of the most common reasons for not completing projects and assignments on time (or ever) is the need to be perfect. If you believe you must create a perfect product (while knowing on some level that nothing is ever perfect), how can you take that first imperfect step? You can't. You're stopped before you even start.

Matrix Thinking:

Here is a tool that you can use to help yourself complete assignments. It's called the matrix. Use a matrix to break down a task into major objectives and individual tasks. Matrix thinking can be used for any assignment. Here's what to do:

1. Describe the assignment in terms of the end result or final product. What is it that you need to do?

2. Identify the major steps that must be taken in order to complete the assignment. These are your intermediate objectives.

3. Identify the specific tasks that must be completed in order to reach each objective.

Assignment: _____

_____

Intermediate Objective:	Intermediate Objective:	Intermediate Objective:
Tasks:	Tasks:	Tasks:

Motivation: It's and Inside Job

Completing assignments or tasks and even achieving goals requires a certain degree of self-motivation. We all work harder when we want to achieve the end result. And, we all have certain things that "push" us to work hard and complete our assignments. It helps if you are aware of what personally motivates you.

Below is a list of common motivators. Check (✔) the ones that apply to you. Since there are many more things that motivate us, see how many you can add to the list.

It is important to understand your motivators and consciously use them whenever you need to motivate yourself to "get the job done."

- • _____ Achievement
- • _____ Influence
- • _____ Interest
- • _____ Status
- • _____ Friendship
- • _____ Money
- • _____ Attention
- • _____ Enjoyment
- • _____ Independence
- • _____ Physical health
- • _____ Security
- • _____ Belonging
- • _____ Competence
- • _____ Authority
- • _____ Praise

_____

_____

_____

_____

_____

_____

Doing What Needs To Be Done: Initiative

Target:

The activities in this section will help you:

⇨ understand why initiative is valued by employers.

⇨ identify skill areas that enable you to take initiative now.

⇨ identify specific tasks requiring initiative and action.

Don't Hold Back — Be the One!

Initiative means the ability to begin or to follow through energetically with a plan or task. It also means taking the first step — being the one to make the opening move. On the job, initiative involves finding and doing things that need to be done without being told to do them. Finding things that need to be done takes alertness and creativity. Doing them takes determination. For these reasons, people who show initiative are highly valued by their teachers and employers, and tend to get ahead faster than those who don't.

One of the most obvious ways you can take initiative is by doing things that involve skills and talents you already possess. For example, if you are good at organizing things, look for ways to improve the organization of your immediate work area. If you're good at troubleshooting computers, offer to help coworkers when they run into problems. If you have an ability to write, contribute to the company newsletter, compose reports, or become the "scribe" for your work team. If you think you need permission first, discuss these ideas with your supervisor before taking action.

What Are You Good At?

1. What do I do especially well? _____

_____

_____

_____

2. What can I do quickly or efficiently? _____

_____

_____

_____

3. What tasks do I enjoy most at home? _____

_____

_____

...school? _____

_____

_____

...work? _____

_____

_____

Once you know what you're especially good at, train yourself to spot tasks that require that skill. Then do those tasks (or volunteer to do them).

What are some things that you could do right now?

_____

_____

_____

_____

How's Your Initiative Now?

Describe a time when you did a chore or a task without being told.

_____

_____

_____

_____

What made you decide to do it? _____

_____

_____

_____

How did other people react? _____

_____

_____

_____

When was the last time you offered someone a helpful suggestion? What was it and how did it occur to you?

_____

_____

_____

Can you think of something you can do right now to demonstrate your initiative? What are some things that come to mind?

_____

_____

_____

_____

Take Responsibility

Have you ever said (or heard someone say), "That's not my job" when faced with a disagreeable or difficult task? Have you ever responded, "It's good enough the way it is" when asked to improve or redo something? The enemy of initiative is being satisfied with mediocre work or "getting by" under current conditions no matter how bad they are.

If you tend to have attitudes like these, work to change them. Strive instead to take responsibility for making things better. Look around at school, at home, in clubs you belong to, or teams you're on. What needs to be done that you could do? Could you:

• organize a storage area
• sort out some books or papers
• clean up a file or a shelf
• make a phone call
• start early on your next assignment
• do some yard work or clean up a room

Make a list of some of the things you can do to demonstrate initiative.

_____   _____
_____   _____
_____   _____
_____   _____
_____   _____
_____   _____
_____   _____
_____   _____

Do It Now!

Nothing impresses as much as immediate follow up. If you say you'll do something, do it now. If you see something that needs to be done, take action right away. Don't waver, falter, vacillate, or procrastinate. When you put things off, they just get worse.

Do it now!

Solving Problems Creatively

Target:

The activities in this section will help you:

➪ assess your current problem-solving ability.

➪ learn a step-by-step process for defining problems and finding solutions that work.

➪ solve a current problem.

➪ increase your problem-solving creativity.

➪ know what to do when a solution doesn't work.

How to Spot a Problem on the Horizon

A problem is a question that must be considered, solved, or answered, such as the problem of how to use a computer software program to organize a particular set of information.

Often the word *problem* is also used to describe a situation or matter (sometimes even a person) that is perplexing or difficult to deal with, such as the problems of traffic congestion and smog, poverty and unemployment, racial prejudice and discrimination.

Though everyone deals with both types of problems, it's the first type — the question that calls for a solution or answer — that you will probably face regularly in your job, just as you do in school. Most of the time, such problems are related to assignments or tasks.

Sometimes work-related problems involve only you. At those times, you need to try and solve the problem yourself, though you can certainly ask for advice. At other times, problems involve coworkers and need to be solved jointly.

Your Problem-Solving Profile

You solve problems practically every day. Many are small. A few are big and complicated. Recall a fairly difficult problem that you solved recently and answer these questions:

1. What was the problem? _____
   _____
   _____

2. Who, besides you, was involved in the problem? _____
   _____

3. How did you go about solving the problem? What steps did you take?
   _____
   _____
   _____

4. How well did the solution work? _____
   _____

5. Is this the process you usually follow when solving problems? If not, describe what you usually do:
   _____
   _____

6. What, for you, is the most difficult thing about trying to find a solution to a problem?

   ____ understanding the problem in the first place

   ____ thinking of things to do

   ____ worrying about whether or not my solution will work

   ____ trying to "sell" my solution to others

   ____ putting my solution into action

Solve Your Problem Step-by-Step

The next time you're faced with a problem, follow the outline below to find a solution. As you proceed through each step of the process, write down your ideas.

1. **Define the problem**
   Sometimes a problem has more than one part. Be sure to define the problem completely (including all parts). If you don't, your solution may not completely eliminate the problem.

2. **Consider asking for help**
   If a problem looks overwhelming, talk it over with someone. Just having someone listen may be enough; or you may want to ask for guidance or advice.

3. **Gather information**
   Write down all the questions you can think of concerning the problem and then start looking for answers. Ask yourself, "Who knows something about this?" Identify sources of information, such as books, manuals, web sites, training videos, people (parent, counselor, teacher, etc.).

4. **Think of possible solutions**
   As you gather information, alternative solutions will start to present themselves. Write them down. Don't stop until you've completely run out of ideas. If your list of alternatives is too limited, go back and increase your pool of information.

5. **Evaluate each alternative**
   Look at each alternative and ask yourself these questions:
   —Will it solve the problem?
   —What are the costs?
   —How do the costs compare to the benefits?

6. **Choose a solution**
   Select the alternative (or a combination) with the best chance of solving the problem. If none of your alternatives seems capable of solving the problem, repeat steps 3 and 4.

7. **Make an implementation plan**
   Write down the exact steps you need to take in order to implement the solution. Put an estimated completion date beside each step.

8. **Implement the solution**
   Do it now. Once you have the solution and the plan, don't waste time worrying about whether or not it will work. Find out.

9. **Evaluate**
   Stick to the solution for a reasonable length of time. If it doesn't work, go back to step 6 and choose a different alternative. If it does work, congratulate yourself!

Solving a Problem

Do you have a problem in your life that needs to be solved? If so, use these three pages to follow the problem-solving steps. If other people are involved in the problem, invite them to go through the steps with you.

1. Define the problem. _____

_____

_____

2. Do I need help? ___ Yes ___ No If yes, from whom?

_____

3. Gather information.
People to ask: _____

_____

Things to read: _____

_____

_____

Places to go: _____

_____

_____

Other: _____

_____

_____

_____

_____

4. List alternative solutions.

	Costs	Benefits
1. _____		
_____		
_____		
2. _____		
_____		
_____		
3. _____		
_____		
_____		
4. _____		
_____		
_____		
5. _____		
_____		
_____		
6. _____		
_____		
_____		
7. _____		
_____		
_____		

5. Evaluate. List costs and benefits next to each alternative.

6. Choose a solution.

(Continued)

7. Make an implementation plan.

	Steps to take:	Completion
Date:		
1. _____		
_____		
2. _____		
_____		
3. _____		
_____		
4. _____		
_____		
5. _____		
_____		

8. Implement the solution.

9. Evaluate.

What worked well and not so well?

_____

_____

_____

_____

_____

_____

_____

_____

_____

_____

_____

_____

Be Creative!

Have you ever felt mentally blocked, completely unable to think of something like a name, date, fact, or solution to a problem — then, hours later, the answer popped into your mind while you were showering, jogging, or walking your dog?

Sometimes your mind can be more creative when you're not forcing it to think logically. Freed from the necessity to think in logical steps, your mind is able to receive messages from the spontaneous, intuitive, artistic part of your brain. Here are some ideas:

• When you're searching for possible solutions, pretend to be an explorer. An explorer doesn't just look in the same tired old places, an explorer ventures bravely into new territory.

• Borrow ideas and methods from different fields. If your job is in the medical field, don't just look in hospitals and doctor's offices for answers. Ask yourself what lawyers, truck drivers, and astronauts do. If your job is in the computer industry, try to think like an artist, farmer, or circus performer.

• Let one thing lead to another. Open your mind and let in ideas that have no obvious connection to the problem you're trying to solve.

• Once you have a list of alternatives, play with them. Compare them. Connect two or more ideas together. Ask yourself "What would happen if...?" Look at each alternative upside down, inside out, and backwards. Then, put the list away for a couple of days and let your unconscious mind play some more — unsupervised.

What To Do When a Solution Isn't Working

When implementing a solution, keep a close watch on the results. Regularly evaluate whether or not the solution is actually solving the problem. If, after a reasonable period of time, you decide the solution is *not* working, abandon that solution and try another. In other words, "cut your losses." Don't keep doing something that isn't working. Instead, invest *future* time in trying a new solution.

How apt are you to "cut your losses" and move on when something's not working? To get an idea, check (✔) your answers to these questions about everyday situations:

• You decide to go to a movie. You buy your ticket and some popcorn, find a seat, and settle back. Forty-five minutes into the movie, you decide that you made a mistake. The movie is really bad. What do you do?
___ get up and walk out
___ suffer through to the end

• You order dinner at a restaurant. When the meal comes, you proceed to taste each item on the plate. You feel disappointed. Nothing is awful, but nothing pleases you either. What do you do?
___ send the dinner back and order something else
___ pick at the food, trying to eat as much as you can
___ stop eating, pay, and leave the restaurant

• In three days, you have a paper due for one of your classes. Every night for a week, you've sat down to your original outline and tried to write different sections. It's not working. The paper is going nowhere. What do you do?
___ keep struggling till you produce the paper, even though it's not very good
___ give up and get a failing grade on the assignment
___ throw away the original outline, develop a new one, and do the best you can in the remaining three days

Knowing when to abandon one solution and try another is a skill that develops with experience and practice. *Don't* try to force-fit solutions that simply aren't working.

Welcoming Criticism and Compliments

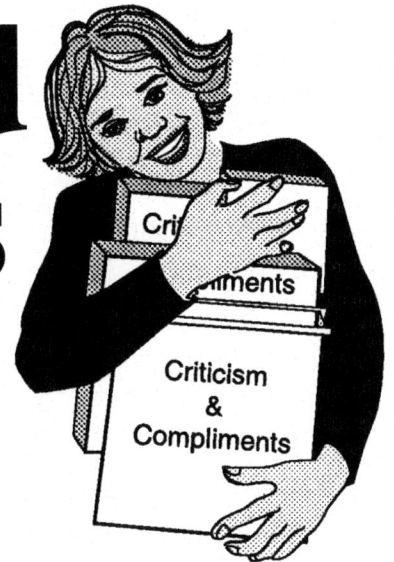

Target:

The activities in this section will help you:

⇨ understand the benefits of compliments and criticism.

⇨ assess your feelings and behaviors as a recipient of compliments and criticism.

⇨ accept compliments easily and gracefully.

⇨ respond to criticism confidently and productively.

Accept Compliments — Take Advantage of Criticism

Compliments and criticism have at least one thing in common. They're both good for you. Compliments tell you what you've done right or well. Knowing that your performance pleased someone gives you the choice to do more of the same. On the other hand, your worst critic can be your best friend. Often when people criticize you, they provide the information you need to improve yourself.

Let people know that you are open to feedback. Take what they have to say, whether pleasing or painful, sort the emotion out of it, and see what you can apply to improve yourself. More often than not, there is at least a grain of truth in the comments of even your harshest critic. Just as there is some truth in the most exaggerated praise.

Enjoy positive feedback. Listen, smile, and let it soak in. You don't have to say anything, but if you feel compelled to speak, limit your response to, "Thank you," "That makes me feel good," or "I really appreciate that."

Ask for negative feedback. Accept the fact that you can always improve and that other people may have some good ideas on how to do so. You can invite criticism by saying something like this: "You seemed to be unhappy with the way I handled _____. If you have a suggestion on how I could have done it better, I'd appreciate it." Do this in a sincere — *never* sarcastic — tone of voice.

Compliments can give you:

- positive reinforcement
- self-esteem
- information about what others like and want
- good feelings
- improved relationships
- energy boosts
- knowledge that you've pleased someone

Criticism can help you:

- learn more about yourself
- become more effective
- measure your performance against company/school expectations
- identify deficiencies that you can work on correcting
- adjust your course, thereby increasing your likelihood of success
- realize that you can't please everyone

Accept Compliments Gracefully

Think of a time recently when someone complimented you. Try to remember how the compliment was worded and write it here:

_____

_____

How did you feel when you were complimented? Check (✔) any that apply.

___ happy   ___ surprised   ___ embarrassed   ___ unworthy
___ flattered   ___ indifferent   ___ self-conscious   ___ other

What did you say? _____

_____

Just Say Thank You

People compliment you on the things they like about you or the things *they believe* you do well. Accept their compliments, even if you don't agree with them. Don't say things like, "Oh, it was nothing" or "Really? I think it's awful." Responding like this not only belittles you, it might make the other person feel a little foolish for complimenting you in the first place.

Learn from Criticism

Now, think of a time recently when someone criticized you. Try to remember exactly what the criticism was. Write it here:

_____

_____

How did you feel when you were criticized? Check (✔) any that apply.

___ indifferent   ___ self-conscious   ___ humiliated   ___ angry
___ confused   ___ embarrassed   ___ picked-on   ___ other
___ interested   ___ alarmed   ___ defensive

What did you say? _____

_____

_____

What did you do? _____

_____

_____

Think of criticism as an opportunity to learn. Criticism lets you know how you (and the things you do) are coming across to other people.

Remember that you *always* have a choice. You can:

1. agree with the criticism, accept it, and do something to change or improve your behavior.

2. disagree with the criticism, reject it, and decide not to change your behavior.

3. accept the criticism and change your behavior even though (in your own mind) you disagree.

You Always Have a Choice!

You always have the freedom to choose how you will react. You can fall apart or become angry — or you can listen and learn. Just because you're not perfect doesn't mean you aren't effective.

Every piece of negative feedback you receive can be of priceless value. Vow to learn from criticism and, if it's valid, do things differently in the future.

How to Respond to Criticism

Listen. This is the hardest part, especially if criticism is accurate. Resist the temptation to interrupt or argue. Control your nonverbal communication, too (facial expressions especially).

Respond positively. Whether the criticism is true or untrue, thank the person for taking the time to bring the matter to your attention.

Ask questions. Get specific information and examples: "What exactly did I do that was careless?" "Which parts of my report were wrong?" "What would you suggest I do differently next time?"

Evaluate. You must decide if the criticism is valid. If it is, accept the fact that you're not perfect, apologize for your mistake, and promise that it won't happen again. If the criticism is not valid, ask questions to find out how the person arrived at this conclusion about you. Don't be defensive. Try to find out what's going on.

Respond. Thank the person for the feedback. If the criticism is valid, take responsibility for what you did. Without putting yourself down, state your intention to improve or change. If the criticism is vague or invalid, you can say simply that you appreciate the feedback and will "think about it." Or say: "Right now I don't agree with you, but I appreciate the feedback and I'll think about it."

Act. If the criticism is correct, immediately develop a plan to change your behavior and improve your performance. Don't waste time making excuses or feeling sorry for yourself. Take action. Do it now!

Assertively Conveying Personal Needs

Target:

The activities in this section will help you:

⇨ recognize your individual human rights.

⇨ distinguish between passive, aggressive, and assertive behaviors.

⇨ increase your ability to behave assertively.

⇨ learn to formulate and make assertive I-statements.

You Have Rights

Try to put away personal concerns before you enter your workplace, and don't take them out again until you leave. For example, if you have an argument with a parent or boyfriend/girlfriend, don't waste time at work talking to coworkers about the situation, and don't make personal phone calls to try and settle the matter during work hours.

Personal concerns that you *do* need to share with your supervisor are those that relate directly to your job performance. By far the best way to convey these concerns is *assertively*.

The ability to assert yourself is more than a way of behaving, it's an attitude, a state of mind. Assertiveness is based on the idea that you have certain rights. For example, you have the right to:
• hold and express opinions and views
• be in charge of your own behavior
• make mistakes
• take chances
• change your mind
• make decisions
• ask questions
• say yes or no without feeling guilty

Three Kinds of Behavior

When people interact with one another, their behavior (words and actions) almost always falls into one of three categories: *passive*, *aggressive*, or *assertive*. Two of these categories — passive and aggressive — should almost always be avoided. Assertive behavior, though it requires time, effort, and patience to learn, is highly effective and worth striving for.

• Passive behavior

This is when you either *don't* express your feelings, opinions, or needs, or when you do so indirectly. When you are passive, you deny your rights and put the responsibility on other people. At work, if you are always passive, people might come to think of you as a wimp. Being passive may cause you to become unhappy and frustrated with yourself, too. Through your words and actions, you send the message, "You are more important than I am" "You win, I lose."

Describe a time when you were passive.

_____

_____

_____

Why did you choose to react this way?

_____

_____

_____

• Aggressive behavior

This is when you express your feelings, opinions, and desires in a threatening, demanding, or hostile manner. You demand your own rights, but deny the rights of others. If you are often aggressive, people will begin to think of you as a "bully." Bullies are cowards pretending to be courageous. They attack, humiliate, and put people down. Bullies send the message, "I'm okay, you're not; I'm right, you're wrong; I have the answers, you don't know anything."

Describe a time when you were aggressive.

_____

_____

_____

Why did you choose to react this way?

_____

_____

_____

• Assertive behavior

This is when you express your feelings, opinions, or needs in an *even* manner that is not hostile or demanding. At the same time, you allow the other person to express him/herself, too. Assertive behavior is honest, direct, and respectful of the rights of others. Its goal is to achieve the kind of win-win solutions that lead to greater trust, confidence, and cooperation among people.

Describe a time when you were assertive.

_____

_____

_____

How did others react? What was the result?

_____

_____

_____

How Did You Respond?

As you've been reading and writing, you've probably thought of situations in which *you* reacted aggressively, passively, or assertively. Perhaps you:

    —wanted someone to leave you alone.

    —were trying to resist a salesperson.

    —wanted to deny someone's request to borrow an item from you.

    —disagreed with someone.

    —wanted to tell someone you were being treated unfairly.

On the chart, briefly describe situations you've experienced, how you felt at the time each situation occurred, whether your behavior was aggressive, passive, or assertive, and how things turned out. Ask yourself: *Could I have been more assertive?*

The Situation	Was Your Behavior Aggressive, Passive, or Assertive	The Outcome

How to Increase Your Assertiveness

Believe in your worth and your rights. Assertive behavior begins inside. It's more than the way you act, it's what you believe. Believe that your opinions count, that you say and do things successfully, that you are in charge of yourself and what happens to you.

Respect others. They have rights, too. While looking out for yourself and asserting your needs, avoid saying or doing anything that infringes on the rights of others. When you do, you cross the line from assertive to aggressive.

Use I-statements. Beginning a statement with the word *I* allows you to express your feelings without attacking the other person. Compare these statements:

You're late again and the whole office is behind schedule. How can you be so irresponsible?

I get really frustrated and the whole office gets frantic and behind schedule when you arrive late. I want to know that you'll be here on time from now on. _____

Turn that awful music off. How do you expect anyone to concentrate!

It's really tough for me to concentrate on my work with your music playing. I'd like you to either find <u>something quieter</u> or turn it off.

You expect me to sit for eight hours in a broken-down chair like that? You must be crazy!

My back hurts when I have to sit in this chair for more than a few minutes. There must be a way that I can get a better chair.

Show your assertiveness nonverbally. In other words, don't let your body language contradict your assertive I-statements. Stand tall yet relaxed. Maintain eye contact. Offer a firm handshake and gesture openly and naturally. Avoid aggressive nonverbal behaviors, like glaring, staring, and pointing with the index finger. Likewise avoid passive behaviors, like chewing on your pencil, twisting your hair, averting your eyes, dropping your head, or limply shaking hands.

I-Statement Tips

To make an I-statement, use this formula:

1. Describe your feelings and/or thoughts

   I feel...

2. Describe the behavior.

   I feel...when you...

3. State why the behavior bothers you.

   I feel...when you... because...

4. Suggest a solution or change of behavior.

   I feel...when you...because.... I would like you to....

Effectively Managing Work-related Conflicts

Target:

The activities in this section will help you:

⇨ understand sources of conflict.

⇨ assess how you typically deal with conflict.

⇨ learn productive conflict-management strategies.

⇨ deal effectively with anger.

⇨ use non-threatening confrontation to define conflicts and put them on the table.

Conflict Happens

There are times in every organization when people disagree. They have different ideas about what should be done and how to do it. They debate an issue, argue about a decision, or bicker over some little detail.

Conflict is normal, and so are the angry feelings that sometimes go with it. Conflict usually means that people have different ideas and that's actually good. The more ideas, the more choices. The trick is to know how to manage conflict, use it to produce good results, and resolve it peacefully.

One of the main sources of work conflict is poor handling of criticism. In the world of work, everyone has a boss. Everyone's performance is judged, and most people receive regular feedback, including formal written evaluations. People *do* get criticized. That's why it's so important to view criticism as an opportunity to learn and grow.

Another major cause of conflict in organizations is change or the threat of change. People become accustomed to working for a particular boss, doing things in certain ways, and following comfortable routines. Then one day the boss is transferred, new procedures are established, the company is reorganized, and old routines are shattered. The inevitable result? Conflict!

How Do You Respond to Conflict?

By taking a look at how you handle conflict situations now, you will be in a better position to control your responses in the future. Use what you learn from answering these questions to set a goal for yourself. What can you do to become a better conflict manager?

I become irritated or annoyed with people who...

_____

I get angry and out of control when...

_____

Why do you think these things or these types of people "push your buttons?"

_____

_____

How do you usually react when something irritates or angers you?

_____

When I have a conflict with someone (like a disagreement or an argument), the first thing I usually do is...

____ lose control   ____ try to calm everyone down
____ clam up   ____ make a joke
____ walk away   ____ listen carefully to the other person's
____ get angry   point of view
____ change the subject   ____ start arguing

Think of a time when you successfully settled a conflict with someone. Describe the conflict and how you resolved it.

_____

_____

_____

_____

_____

How to Resolve a Conflict

When you find yourself in a conflict, don't waste energy on hate, envy, or dreams of revenge. Resolve it! Realize and appreciate that people are different, with conflicting priorities and points of view. *You* are in charge of how you react to conflict. You can fall apart, become consumed with rage, or get to work finding a solution to the problem.

Conflict Resolution Strategies

Depending on the nature of the conflict and who the conflict is with, you can use one or more of these strategies to help resolve it.

1. **Share**

   Whatever the conflict is over, keep (or use) some of it yourself, and let the other person have or use some.

2. **Take turns**

   Use or do something for a little while. Then let the other person take a turn.

3. **Active listen**

   Let the other person talk while you listen carefully. Really try to understand the person's feelings and ideas.

4. **Postpone**

   If you or the other person are very angry or tired, put off dealing with the conflict until another time.

5. **Get help**

   Not every conflict can or should be resolved by the parties involved. Sometimes you need to ask a third party to act as a mediator. This should be a neutral person who listens well.

6. **Use humor**

   Look at the situation in a comical way. Don't take it too seriously.

7. **Compromise**

   Offer to give up part of what you want and ask the other person to do the same.

8. **Walk away**

   Some conflicts aren't worth getting involved in. When you are outnumbered, feel physically threatened, or find yourself in the middle of a conflict that you don't want any part of, leave.

9. **Express regret**

   Say that you are sorry about the situation, without taking the blame.

10. **Problem solve**

    Discuss the problem and try to find a solution that is acceptable to both you and the other person.

Controlling Anger

Annoyance and anger are very normal reactions. You have a choice when you feel angry, because *you* control your behavior. You don't have to show your anger. You can handle those feelings productively.

When people are rude to you, it may not be because of something you have done to them. Try not to take it personally. Thoughtless, rude people are often in a bad mood over something that occurred before they made contact with you. Remind yourself that you probably had nothing to do with the cause.

When someone makes a hostile comment, try to defuse the situation. Refuse to allow your own button to be pushed. Give an appropriate response or take a corrective action. See if you can figure out how to say or do something to improve the situation.

Anger is often a *secondary* emotion. That means that some *other* emotion comes right before the anger. For example, imagine being on a worksite and a senior coworker criticizes you in front of a customer, your first feeling is probably embarrassment or humiliation. However, anger overtakes and engulfs that first feeling so fast that you may never even recognize it. When you blow up at the coworker, fury is all that comes across. How much better it would be to let the coworker know that what he or she did was disrespectful because it embarrassed or humiliated you. It isn't easy, but try to catch and express that first feeling:

I felt embarrassed when...

I felt humiliated when...

I was worried because...

I get extremely frustrated when...

I felt overwhelmed by...

I feel confused when...

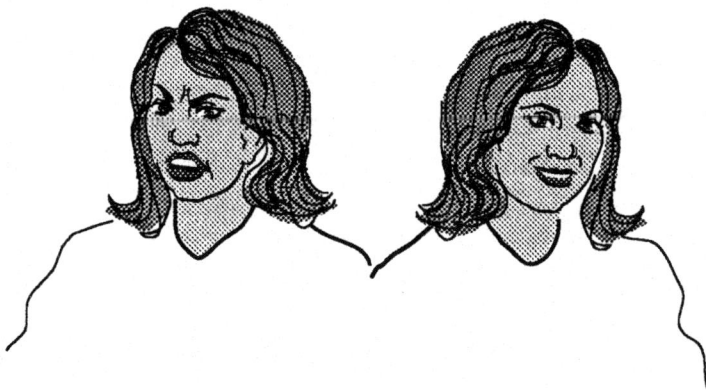

Observing and Learning from Conflicts

     Keep your eyes and ears open for conflict. It probably won't take long before you observe two or more people having a disagreement of some kind. Don't get involved; however, if you can, pay attention. Then, as soon as possible after the conflict has ended, write down your answers to the following questions. After you have observed at least two conflicts and written about them, use another piece of paper to write down what you've learned about handling conflicts.

What was the conflict about?	What was the conflict about?
_____	_____
_____	_____
_____	_____
How many people were involved?	How many people were involved?
_____	_____
Describe what happened:	Describe what happened:
_____	_____
_____	_____
_____	_____
_____	_____
Check (✔) all methods that were used to resolve or end the conflict:	Check (✔) all methods that were used to resolve or end the conflict:
___ fight or argument	___ fight or argument
___ putting it off	___ putting it off
___ walking away	___ walking away
___ apologizing	___ apologizing
___ sharing or taking turns	___ sharing or taking turns
___ humor	___ humor
___ compromise	___ compromise
___ asking for help	___ asking for help
___ problem solving or negotiation	___ problem solving or negotiation
___ other (describe below)	___ other (describe below)

Confrontation — Putting a Conflict on the Table

Lots of conflicts live underground. You can't see them exactly, but you can sense them. Sometimes two people can work alongside each other for months or even years in a state of unacknowledged conflict. This kind of situation is stressful not just for the people directly involved, but for everyone around them. A common reason for not dealing directly with conflict is the fear of confrontation.

Confrontation always occurs in the open. You can't hide or deny a conflict and confront it at the same time. Confronting a conflict usually involves confronting the other person — telling the other person what is bothering you or the points on which you disagree. Confrontation is a necessary first step to conflict resolution because it *defines* the conflict.

One of the most effective ways to confront a conflict is by combining two techniques: *I-statements* and *active listening*. Here is how they work

---

1. Use the <u>I-statement</u> to make your point, voice your concern, or express your disagreement.

   I have the feeling that you disagree with the way I'm doing this. I think we should talk about it.

   I have a big problem with this procedure. I don't think it's going to work and I think we should reconsider.

   I resent it when you use my ideas and don't give me credit for them. I think it's affecting my ability to work with you and we need to discuss it.

2. Then shift to <u>active listening</u> as the other person responds.

   ...So you're saying that you don't disagree totally, but you do think I've made some mistakes.

   ...Then you really believe that this procedure will work and we should give it more time.

   ...So you don't think you've ever intentionally done that — used my ideas.

3. Once the other person has expressed his or her opinion, make another I-statement.

4. Listen actively again.

5. Continue this pattern until the conflict has been defined. Then start the problem-solving process, or use one of the other conflict-resolution strategies (see earlier page).

Becoming a Trusted Employee

Target:

The activities in this section will help you:

⇨ understand the components of trust and how trust is developed.

⇨ assess your own beliefs and experiences about trust.

⇨ examine common on-the-job behaviors that tend to destroy trust.

⇨ build trusting relationships.

How Trust Is Earned

When starting a new job, it takes at least a week to receive your first paycheck. The money is earned by completing the work assigned to you. It can take a lot longer to earn the trust of your employer. Doing your assigned work contributes a great deal to the trust-building process; however, much more is involved. Here are four standards of ethical conduct that together build trust:

Honesty: Tell the truth. Be sincere. Don't betray the trust of your employer; mislead, deceive or trick your customers. Don't withhold important information (on applications and in interviews, for example). Don't take things that don't belong to you.

Integrity: Stand up for your beliefs about right and wrong. Do what you say you are going to do. Show commitment and self-discipline.

Promise-keeping: Keep your word, honor your commitments, and meet your deadlines. When you borrow an item from a coworker, return it promptly.

Loyalty: Stand by and support the people who are important to you, including your employer. Don't talk behind people's backs, spread rumors or participate in harmful gossip. Don't ask a coworker to do something wrong.

Where Do You Stand on Trust?

Take a few minutes to explore your own thoughts and feelings about trust. As you answer these questions, think about how your experiences and feelings can be applied to a job setting.

Think of a person you really trust. What does this person do to earn your trust?

_____

_____

Now, think of someone you totally *mistrust*. Why don't you trust this person?

_____

_____

How do you feel when you find out someone has lied to you?

_____

When you lie to a friend or family member, do you still expect that person to trust you? Why or why not?

_____

How did you feel the last time a person broke a promise or commitment to you? What effect did the incident have on your relationship with this person?

_____

Can you recall a time when you found out that someone was spreading gossip about you behind your back? What happened to your trust for those involved?

_____

In order to be a more trustworthy person, what aspects of trust — honesty, integrity, promise-keeping, or loyalty — do you most need to work on? How will you do it?

_____

_____

_____

Building Trusting and Caring Relationships

Establishing good relationships with others, whether it's in the workplace, at school, on teams, in organizations, or even in the family, begins with showing others that they can trust you and that you care about them.

Trust and caring are the basis of all good relationships, and establishing strong and healthy relationships in all parts of life is an important aspect of school, work, and life success.

How well do you demonstrate trust and caring in your relationships? Here is a checklist of good behaviors. Check (✔) the ones that you naturally engage in. If you don't check some items, it will give you a good idea of what skills and values you can improve upon.

_____ I'm aware that others need to know they can count on me. If I say I will do something, I'll do it.

_____ I don't criticize, share secrets, or gossip behind people's backs.

_____ I listen to others with genuine interest. I appreciate their ideas and interests, and show concern for their problems.

_____ I make sure that my body language also shows my interest. I look at and face the person who is talking. and I use an open and receptive body stance.

_____ When others are speaking, I don't interrupt and take the focus away from them. I fully listen to others by letting them finish their thoughts before adding my own.

If your heart is in Social-Emotional
Learning, visit us online.

Come see us at
www.InnerchoicePublishing.com

Our web site gives you a look at all our other Social-Emotional
Learning-based books, free activities, articles, research, and
learning and teaching strategies. Every week you'll get a new
Sharing Circle topic and lesson.

INNERCHOICE Publishing
15079 Oak Chase Court
Wellington, FL 33414

CPSIA information can be obtained
at www.ICGtesting.com
Printed in the USA
FSOW04n2356200515
7219FS

9 781564 990716